YOUR SWASH IS UNBUCKLED

A collection of stage combat plays

By Jeff Goode

Baker's Plays
7611 Sunset Blvd.
Los Angeles, CA 90042
BAKERSPLAYS.COM

NOTICE

This book is offered for sale at the price quoted only on the understanding that, if any additional copies of the whole or any part are necessary for its production, such additional copies will be purchased. The attention of all purchasers is directed to the following: This work is protected under the copyright laws of the United States of America, in the British Empire, including the Dominion of Canada, and all other countries adhering to the Universal Copyright Convention. Violations of the Copyright Law are punishable by fine or imprisonment, or both. The copying or duplication of this work or any part of this work, by hand or by any process, is an infringement of the copyright and will be vigorously prosecuted.

This play may not be produced by amateurs or professionals for public or private performance without first submitting application for performing rights. Royalties are due on all performances whether for charity or gain, or whether admission is charged or not. Since performance of this play without the payment of the royalty fee renders anybody participating liable to severe penalties imposed by the law, anybody acting in this play should be sure, before doing so, that the royalty fee has been paid. Professional rights, reading rights, radio broadcasting, television and all mechanical rights, etc. are strictly reserved. Application for performing rights should be made directly to BAKER'S PLAYS.

No one shall commit or authorize any act or omission by which the copyright of, or the right to copyright, this play may be impaired. No one shall make any changes in this play for the purpose of production.

Publication of this play does not imply availability for performance. Both amateurs and professionals considering a production are strongly advised in their own interest to apply to Baker's Plays for written permission before starting rehearsals, advertising, or booking a theatre.

Whenever the play is produced, the author's name must be carried in all publicity, advertising and programs. Also, the following notice must appear on all printed programs, "Produced by special arrangement with Baker's Plays."

Licensing fees for *YOUR SWASH IS UNBUCKLED* is based on a per performance rate and payable one week in advance of the production.
Please consult the Baker's Plays website at www.bakersplays.com or our current print catalogue for up to date licensing fee information.

YOUR SWASH IS UNBUCKLED
ISBN **978-0-87440-291-9**   # 1715-B

YOUR SWASH IS UNBUCKLED is a collection of short stage combat plays designed to showcase the work of fight choreographers and combatants.

The plays in this collection can be performed as stand-alone theatre pieces, or grouped together to create an evening of theatre.

Any production of three or more of these pieces should be performed under the title Your Swash is Unbuckled by Jeff Goode.

ABOUT THE PLAYWRIGHT

Jeff Goode is a producer, director and screenwriter, and the author of over 50 plays, musicals and children's shows, including the international hit *The Eight: Reindeer Monologues*. He created the animated television series *American Dragon: Jake Long* for the Disney Channel. You can find him on the web at: www.jeffgoode.com

YOUR SWASH IS UNBUCKLED opened July 19, 2007, at the Iowa Fringe Festival, a production of Rage Theatrics.

JOLLY JACK JUNIOR:
THE BUCCANEER'S BAIRN
Directed by Scott Lewis

Fight choreography by Nate Mims

CECILY JACK. . . . . Nancy Mayfield

PIRATE WILLY . . . . Nate Mims

LEWD LOVES OF A LUSTY LAUNDRESS
Directed by Kate C. Thompson

Fight choreography by Jason Tipsword

MOLLY . . . . Becca Miller

BERTHABELLA . . . . Jason Tipsword

POLYNESIA. . . . . Aaron Haworth

STEPMOTHER . . . . Nate Kula

BRIDGET OF BRISTOL:
THE BAWDY BRIGANDESS
Directed by Nancy Mayfield

Fight choreography by Jason Tipsword

BRIDGET. . . . . Kate C. Thompson

DAMSEL. . . . . Megan Sands

Sound scallywag . . . . Peter Birk

TABLE OF CONTENTS

With undying gratitude to

Ian Allen
(Cherry Red Productions)

Jennifer Shepard
(ImprovAcadia)

and

the talented combatants of
RAGE THEATRICS

for their inspiration,
perspiration,
and collaboration

LEWD LOVES OF A
LUSTY LAUNDRESS

*(A medieval laundry. Sounds of revelry in the distance.
Enter **MOLLY** with a bundle of clothes.)*

MOLLY. Everyone else is going to the fair. But do I get to
go? No, I do not. I have to scrub the floor and clean
the stable and hang the laundry out to dry while my
wicked stepmother and my two horrible stepsisters go
to the fair. Just like Cinderella. *(grumbles)* An' I wish I
was like Cinderella and could have a handsome prince
come save me from my suffering. Or not even a prince
– any able-bodied man will do.

(Dream music – perhaps a harp.)

Aye, any handsome virile rake on a white stallion with
rippling muscles – the rake, not the stallion – who
would carry me away from this drudgery to a life of
sensuous adventure. *(She lapses into romantic reverie.)* He
comes to me like a thief in the night. Stealing to my
bedside, he speaks to me of forbidden pleasures. And
when he whispers my name, the words fall from his
chiseled lips like drops of molten honey –

MANLY VOICE. *(offstage)* Molly! Molly MacGregor!

MOLLY. Yes, my love!

MANLY VOICE. Your love? Are ye daft, girl? It's me, Berthabella, your horrible stepsister.

*(Enter **BERTHABELLA**, her horrible, yet manly, stepsister.)*

ANOTHER MANLY VOICE. *(offstage)* And Polynesia!

MOLLY. My other horrible stepsister.

*(Enter **POLYNESIA**, her other manly stepsister, playing
a harp.)*

BERTHABELLA. Would you stop playing that blasted harp, Polynesia? It drives me crazy!

(Harp music stops.)

Have you finished with the laundry yet, Molly? There's a frock I want to wear to the fair.

POLYNESIA. Yes, and my sunbonnet, I want it.

MOLLY. I'm just now hangin' them out to dry.

BERTHABELLA. Well, see that you do. We want to look lovely when we go to the fair.

POLYNESIA. In case we meet our future husbands there.

MOLLY. Someday, I shall have a husband. And he shall take me away from this place. And then you will have to do your own laundry.

BERTHABELLA. Oh!

POLYNESIA. Mother!

*(Molly's manly **STEPMOTHER** enters.)*

STEPMOTHER. What is it?!

POLYNESIA. Molly is threatening us with housework again.

STEPMOTHER. Are you having delusions of escaping your pathetic life of labor again, Molly?

MOLLY. Yes, stepmother.

STEPMOTHER. What have I told you about that?

MOLLY. *(petulant)* I don't know.

STEPMOTHER. *(to the Stepsisters)* Girls?

BERTHABELLA & POLYNESIA. "That dreams don't come true, for lasses like you!"

STEPMOTHER. *(to the Stepsisters)* Now get yourselves ready, we're going to the fair.

MOLLY. Stepmother, may I go to the fair, too?

BERTHABELLA & POLYNESIA. No!!

MOLLY. Please?

STEPMOTHER. When you've finished all the laundry, *then* you may go to the fair, and not a moment before.

MOLLY. But, I am almost finished, this is the last of it.

STEPMOTHER. Oh, didn't I tell you? We took in extra this morning.

*(**POLYNESIA** brings in a gigantic bundle of laundry, throws it down in front of **MOLLY**.)*

STEPMOTHER. When *that's* done, you can go to the fair.

(Stepfamily exits, laughing uproariously.)

MOLLY. I'll never be done with this in time. Stepmother is right. I guess I'm just not the kind of lass to have her dreams come true.

*(**MOLLY** starts going through the new bundle of laundry.)*

Look at this. Shirts and stockings, and more shirts, and boots to polish, and what's this?

*(**MOLLY** pulls an expensive shirt from the bundle.)*

A shirt fair belonging to a lord. Aye, an' a mighty Scottish lord, at that. *(fantasizing)* With tousled hair, all covered with mail. His sinewy chest gleaming in the moonlight. He'll spirit me away to his keep high in the Scottish hills where I'll be slave to his every desire.

*(**MOLLY** takes another shirt from the bundle. It is a princely shirt, trimmed with lace.)*

And what have we here? A prince's shirt, I think. A handsome, brave prince, with steely blue eyes to gaze into. He has a pair of wide shoulders and strong arms to crush me in his embrace when he gallantly carries me off to his castle and there entreats me to be his queen.

*(**MOLLY** takes another shirt from the bundle. It's a pirate shirt.)*

And this one's a pirate's shirt. Stolen at swordpoint from a wealthy silk trader. I can see him, I can, handsome and bold with dancing brown eyes, curly brown hair, lean and muscular with a cutlass in his hand.

MANLY VOICE. *(offstage)* Molly! Molly MacGregor!

MOLLY. *(snapping back to reality)* Aye, stepsister, I'll have your frock in a bit.

(But it's not Berthabella – Enter a **PIRATE**. *He is not wearing a shirt.)*

PIRATE. Arr, lass, what care I for frocks? What I desire from you only your nubile body can yield.

MOLLY. Who are you?

PIRATE. Why, I'm the dread pirate, handsome and bold, lean and muscular, come to free you from your cruel suffering, only to lash you in silken bonds of forbidden love.

MOLLY. *(simultaneously)* …come to free me from my cruel suffering, only to lash me in silken bonds of forbidden love?

PIRATE. How did you know?

MOLLY. This must be a dream.

PIRATE. *(passionately)* If this be a dream, let me never wake again. I'll take you aboard my ship. We'll sail the straits of passion. Adrift on the throbbing seas, our feverish bodies entwined in a net of intoxicating ecstasy.

MOLLY. *(joining in)* …Adrift on the throbbing seas, our feverish bodies entwined in a net of intoxicating ecstasy.

MOLLY. I knew it! And if I refuse? Will you hold me captive to your desire, till my resistance melts under your searing caress?

PIRATE. *(thinks about it)* …Okay.

MOLLY. *(leaping into his arms)* "No, no," I will cry, in defense of my maiden modesty, though I ache to feel your hot breath upon my bosom. Torn between doubt and desire, heaving and panting, I collapse into your powerful arms, as you abduct me to your dark pirate cave, where at last, unwilling, I submit to your manly advances.

(He starts to do just that.)

Or, no, not a cave... A secret lagoon. Or a tropical island!

PIRATE. I have both.

MOLLY. *(joyfully)* Oh yes! *(then playing her part)* I mean: "No! I shall resist you, arrogant buccaneer!"

PIRATE. Resist this!

> (**PIRATE** *kisses her. She melts. Enter a* **PRINCE,** *also shirtless.*)

PRINCE. What ho, ye brigand! Unhand that breathtaking enchantress.

MOLLY. *(to* **PRINCE***)* Not just yet.

PIRATE. Who's that?

PRINCE. The dashing prince, handsome and brave. Do you like the way the sun glints on my muscular chest?

MOLLY. *(to* **PIRATE***)* He's come to rescue me from your sinister clutches.

PRINCE. That's right.

MOLLY. *(rushing into his arms)* He'll gather me in his arms, and safe within his strong, yet tender embrace, I'll ride off with him to his glittering palace. There he will lavish me with gifts and entreat me to be his queen.

PIRATE. *(taking her back)* But what about me? I awakened desires you never knew. Can you so soon forget the nights of cruel passion we shared?

MOLLY. *(trying to decide)* Shall I renounce my throne to lead a life of violent seduction? Or forsake his desire to follow my destiny: a life of lavish sensuousness and the intrigues of the court.

PRINCE. I vote the court.

PIRATE. I say violent seduction.

MOLLY. Oh, I know! The two of you have to fight over me.

> *(They violently hurl themselves at each other.)*

No, no, not like that.

> *(She stops them and rearranges them more artfully.)*

Here, with me on your arm, like this.

(She hangs from one of the PIRATE's arms as the fight begins again.)

Save me, my prince, from this vulgar outlaw!

(She switches over to the PRINCE's arm.)

If you survive, my love, I will lie in your arms tonight, consumed by fiery passions I cannot contain. We will soar to new heights of love.

(MOLLY flings herself onto the PIRATE.)

Please, spare him, I beg you, and I will go with you, pleasing you in all things, my body a mere toy for you to use as you wish, if you will only let him live.

(to the audience)

But alas, neither man heeded her words, and the fight went on and on for the hand of the fair maiden, neither man willing to surrender. Life without her at their side would be worse than any death. Their muscles rippled as they fought, their chests heaved. The only sound the two men made was their labored breathing as each struggled to best the other. In the hot midday heat they thrust and parried, and then parried and thrust, in and out, out and in, steel blades flashed in the sunlight, the sweat glistened on their bodies. Stop, stop, you've got to stop.

(She comes between them, trying to catch her breath.)

Okay, just a bit more.

(They fight a bit more.)

In, out, lunge, thrust. Oh!

(Coming between them again)

That's good, stop, stop.

(After a brief pant, she resumes)

I cannot allow you to harm this handsome, bold prince. Nor apprehend this daring pirate.

(Enter the **SCOTTISH LORD.***)*

SCOTTISH LORD. There you are! From my home in the Scottish highlands I've heard tales of your beauty, Molly MacGregor. And I've come now to take you off to my keep.

MOLLY. I wasn't quite done with these two.

SCOTTISH LORD. *(seizing her)* Come, you alluring vixen, I've risked all to possess you.

MOLLY. With ruffian lust the Scottish lord woos me.

SCOTTISH LORD. *(taking the hint)* Woo.

MOLLY. Harder.

SCOTTISH LORD. WOO!

MOLLY. I mean, more eloquently.

SCOTTISH LORD. Och! What care I for eloquence? You'll come with me now, or I will ravish you on the spot.

MOLLY. Even better.

PRINCE. I'm afraid that's my queen, you're seducing.

PIRATE. And mine.

PRINCE. Pirates don't have queens.

PIRATE. My booty then.

SCOTTISH LORD. I've crossed mountains and conquered armies to possess this tender virgin. And I shall vanquish, any man who stands against me!

(They fight. **MOLLY** *cheers them on.)*

PIRATE. *(suddenly feeling something in his loins)* Whooa!

PRINCE. What is it?

PIRATE. I just felt a quickening in my loins.

PRINCE. *(as he turns toward* **MOLLY***)* Whooa! I feel it too.

PIRATE. It's the girl!!

(They both look at the **SCOTTISH LORD** *who is still waiting for his loins to quicken.)*

PRINCE. Looks like yours is on the blink.

(The **SCOTTISH LORD** *bellows and attacks them, and the fight is on again. After awhile, the* **PIRATE** *is killed.)*

MOLLY. Dread Pirate Handsome-and-Bold!

(MOLLY is too far away from the PIRATE when he dies, so she stops the fight.)

Wait!

(She runs over to the PIRATE.)

And with a dying kiss, that lingers on my lips, and a burning look of tender yearning in his eyes, he tragically departs this world.

(PIRATE drops dead.)

Okay.

(The fight continues. The SCOTTISH LORD kills the PRINCE.)

No, no, just wound him, there's already one dead. You want me to get a complex?

(The PRINCE gets up and fights again, but this time the SCOTTISH LORD only disables him.)

No, actually, the prince should win.

(The PRINCE gets up and fights again, disarming and defeating the SCOTTISH LORD. MOLLY rushes to the PRINCE's side.)

Both wicked men felled by his sword, the prince at last claims his prize.

PRINCE. C'mere, prize!

(They are about to kiss, when:)

MANLY VOICE. *(offstage)* Molly! Molly MacGregor!

(The PRINCE vanishes, as BERTHABELLA comes in.)

BERTHABELLA. Have you finished with my frock?

MOLLY. In a minute.

BERTHABELLA. Well, hurry up!

(BERTHABELLA leaves. MOLLY looks around at the empty stage, scattered with laundry. No princes, no pirates.)

MOLLY. It was only a dream, a fantasy.

(Beat. She looks down at the **SCOTTISH LORD,** *who is still lying there.)*

So, why are you here?

SCOTTISH LORD. *(sitting up)* Oh, I'm real.

MOLLY. You are?

SCOTTISH LORD. Yep.

MOLLY. You really are a Scottish lord from the highlands?

SCOTTISH LORD. Yep.

MOLLY. And you're going to sweep me away to your secret stronghold?

SCOTTISH LORD. And love you as no other.

MOLLY. With hot hands to possess and caress me?

SCOTTISH LORD. And thrill you with sensuous delights.

MOLLY. Why didn't you say so before?!

SCOTTISH LORD. Shall I take you to new heights of passion?

MOLLY. Okay, but first, take me to the fair.

SCOTTISH LORD. Of course, my love.

(They kiss.)

Whooa! There it goes.

(They exit together.)

FIN

BRIDGET OF BRISTOL:
THE BAWDY BRIGANDESS
IN
"THE DAMSEL AND THIS DRESS"

(A raucous pub. A **FEMALE BRIGAND** *leaps up on a table with a rapier in one hand and a tankard of ale in the other.)*

BRIGANDESS. Listen hard, ye blackguards! And by "hard", I mean "well". And by "well" I mean, with your lips a-button, for once, that a lady may get a word in, for I've heard enough braggardry tonight to last a lass a lifetime.

But the true measure of a man is in his mettle. And by "metal", I mean his blade. And by "blade" I *don't* mean his manhood. So ye may keep your pricks in your drawers, and prick up your swords, for there's a pint of ale in it for any man can best me with his prowess. And a prick of mine own for any man can't.

And lest ye take me for an easy tankard, I'll warn ye fair: I am none other than the notorious Bridget of Chitbridge, the Fair Brigand of Bristol – the finest swordsman ever wore corset and heels. Not counting, of course, Sir Gaylord of Flouncy, for he's quick with a dirk in a frock, but that's a story for another time. For the time being, all you need know is there's not one man in ten thousand can match me for steel or for wit. And I don't see ten thousand men here.

Now who's for me? Or shall I drink to mine own health and be done?

(A **COURTLY DAMSEL** *springs up to challenge her.)*

DAMSEL. You'll be done indeed, when I'm done with ye. Though you won't have half so much health to drink to.

BRIGANDESS. Big words for a wee damsel. Now, begone with ye, girl. You're interfering in men's business.

DAMSEL. Men's business ye may be, but your business tonight is with me.

BRIGANDESS. 'Od's Bollix! I've ne'er seen such churlish swagger in such a girlish figure. What woman are ye that dares defy the She-Pistol of East Bristol?

DAMSEL. I am none other than the woman whose fiancé you deprived of his manhood, not two weeks ago, on the high road to Bristol. And I mean to have it back!

BRIGANDESS. Not meaning to be graphic, young milady, but if it's been two weeks since your man's seen his manhood, I don't think you *want* it back. We've had a spot of rain lately, and the ditches get dewy.

DAMSEL. I mean, his blade, you russet hussy! That bejeweled ancestral heirloom which his family has handed down from father to son, to father to son, to father to pawnbroker to mother-in-law back to son, for more generations than you can count.

BRIGANDESS. So, more than three?

DAMSEL. And don't try to deny ye've ta'en it for I see it plainly there in your hand – the family jewel-studded rapier – reft of my prince's rightful possession, when you set upon him in the forest, and overwhelmed him with your naughty minions.

BRIGANDESS. I remember your prince, now you mention him. But if he told you there were minions, the man's as perjured as an orient rug, for I work alone.

DAMSEL. I don't mean to doubt you, but the prince is a lofty man. And by "lofty," I mean "tall." And strapping as a thoroughbred stallion. How would a woman alone have waylaid him in the wood?

BRIGANDESS. That's kind of a personal question, don't you think?

DAMSEL. He told me you beset him with masked minions –

BRIGANDESS. There were no minions.

DAMSEL. – robbed him, reviled him, and left him unarmed, unhorsed and unpantsed on the high road to Bristol, without even his pride to comfort him on the cold road home.

BRIGANDESS. Well, if it's the same prince I'm thinkin' of, he was indeed strapped like a stallion, and the pride alone should have kept him warm.

DAMSEL. That's what I tried to tell him! But it's no use, the man is distraught, and there's naught I've said or done – or fondled – since, has rekindled his injured esteem.

BRIGANDESS. Did you try giving him pants?

DAMSEL. I gave him pants! But no taut set of breeches can replace the loss of that which his grandmother fought so hard to regain – the family's manhood. And she's going to be at the wedding, so we really need it back. Now unhand my Prince's instrument, or it shall be the instrument of your own undoing.

BRIGANDESS. I admire your spunk – and your imagery – but did you not hear me the first time? There's not a man in ten thousand can match wits with my steel.

DAMSEL. Aye, but is there a *woman*?

BRIGANDESS. Argh! I should have seen that one coming. A curse o' my third grade education!

DAMSEL. I, on the other hand, attended a four-year college, and mastered all manner of courtly arts.

BRIGANDESS. Well, unless one of those arts was fencing –

(The DAMSEL lunges to the attack.)

BRIGANDESS. Oh, it *was* fencing!

(They fight. The DAMSEL disarms the BRIGANDESS and holds her at swordpoint.)

BRIGANDESS. You're not bad for a damsel.

DAMSEL. And you're not good for a professional bandit. You say you do this for a living?

BRIGANDESS. Alas, I have not your skill at swordplay, for I was raised a poor peasant girl. So I only learned to fight dirty!

(She hurls her ale in the **DAMSEL***'s face and lunges to the counterattack. They fight. They fall to wrestling. The* **BRIGANDESS** *pins the* **DAMSEL***.)*

DAMSEL. Well, it seems you're skilled, after all, in your own way.

BRIGANDESS. It comes of having eight older brothers. And four younger uncles. They taught me everything I know – the hard way.

DAMSEL. It's too bad ye hadn't any sisters.

BRIGANDESS. Why's that?

DAMSEL. They might have taught ye this:

(The **DAMSEL** *pulls her hair. She fights inappropriately – use your imagination. The* **DAMSEL** *defeats her foe and regains her sword.)*

DAMSEL. Have you any last words?

BRIGANDESS. No, I'm more of a screamer.

DAMSEL. Then prepare to pay for the wrongs I have suffered.

(The **DAMSEL** *attacks.)*

BRIGANDESS. The wrongs *you've* suffered?? I had to go to a public school!

DAMSEL. Your piteous history moves me almost to clemency. But I cannot soon forget that you robbed the man I love of that which is rightly mine as his future wife to deprive him – his masculine dignity.

BRIGANDESS. Aye, but only after he tried to rob me of that which is no man's right to lay hands on – my feminine innocence.

DAMSEL. Your what?

BRIGANDESS. You heard me, and don't laugh. He sought to sully my maiden virtue. I said, don't laugh. All right, stop laughing.

DAMSEL. You! A maiden?!

BRIGANDESS. Aye, a maiden, I!

DAMSEL. But look at how you're dressed.

BRIGANDESS. What's wrong with the way I'm dressed?

DAMSEL. Not meaning to offend, but in that outfit, you're quite fetching.

BRIGANDESS. Thank'ee. None taken.

DAMSEL. No, I mean it, you're comely as a shepherd's first ewe. No chaste woman would be caught dead in that outfit – lest she be chased and caught live and soon violated by the first man she meets. And then spurned ever after by every man since for being damaged goods.

BRIGANDESS. Why d'ye think I carry a rapier?

DAMSEL. I don't mean to disparage your character, for 'tis unladylike – your character, I mean – but, honestly, that dress is asking for it.

BRIGANDESS. Indeed? Well, your future husband did his best to satisfy this dress.

DAMSEL. How dare you!

BRIGANDESS. How dare he!

DAMSEL. I have made allowances, till now, for your rude upbringing, but you go too far! The prince would ne'er have tainted so much as his nether lip with the likes of thee.

BRIGANDESS. Then how do you explain this?

(She grabs her, and kisses her.)

DAMSEL. *(swooning)* My prince… *(realizing)* My God! You kiss like the prince!!

BRIGANDESS. He taught me things I didn't know you could learn with your mouth.

DAMSEL. O woe is me! My beloved has betrayed my honour by besmirching *his* honour by bespoiling yours. Not that you had much to begin with, but it's the thought that counts. O, I am ruined. Ruined! If you have any mercy, slay me now, and spare me the life of shameful ill-repute, which you yourself must know, having given yourself to the same man. And in that outfit.

BRIGANDESS. Ye may save the hysterics for your wedding night, for I gave myself to no man. I may have kissed a prince in the wood, as any wench would, but I am a maiden still!

DAMSEL. Then my love has not been betrayed?

BRIGANDESS. Not all the way, at least.

DAMSEL. But that's impossible! How could a common girl of common birth resist a prince of noble girth – I mean, birth.

BRIGANDESS. No, it was the girth that almost got me. And don't think I wasn't tempted. Every peasant girl dreams of succumbing to a man of his ilk. Strapped like he was. And armed to the hilt. ...But then I saw this!

(She holds up her hand.)

DAMSEL. Your hand?

BRIGANDESS. The ring.

(There is a jeweled ring on her finger.)

DAMSEL. Wait a moment, that's *my* ring! The one I gave the prince as a token of our troth.

BRIGANDESS. I saw this ring, and then I knew the prince would never love me true, for he had sworn his love to you. And so it was, with heavy hearts – and certain heavy other parts – we parted ways there in that wood. He with his honour, and me with his sword.

DAMSEL. Wait. What? Why did he give you the sword?

BRIGANDESS. You're right, that story doesn't make any sense. Let me think...

DAMSEL. O, for the love of St. Blarney! You *did* succumb to his temptations!

BRIGANDESS. No! I beat back his advances. I swear it on my maidenhead!

(She claps her hand over her heart. She quickly realizes that's the wrong place, and moves it.)

DAMSEL. Hah! You are no more a maiden than I am a scullery mop. For I majored in equestrian studies, and beating a stallion only drives him on!

BRIGANDESS. It wasn't like that! You must believe me!

DAMSEL. Ye may cease your protestations for I need no more proof than this: If he kissed you the way you say he did, your heart must have raced, your bosom must have heaved, your breath must have caught in your corset, as it does even now at the mere memory of his courtly caress!

BRIGANDESS. O, it did! It does! The thought of his rough touch incites my blood to seethe with desires only a man of noble carriage – and not insubstantial undercarriage – can soothe.

DAMSEL. I knew your story smelt of fish!

BRIGANDESS. Alright, I admit it! I submitted to his wishes right there in Bristol's ditches. I gave myself to him, as any red-blooded American girl would do in my boots.

DAMSEL. Aye, those Americans are harlots.

BRIGANDESS. And they like boots. But, alas, my moment of wanton weakness was short-lived, for ere I could reach that summit of passion which no man can attain – but it takes a man to get you there…

DAMSEL. …Yes? …Yes??

BRIGANDESS. The handsome prince, to my chagrin, exhausted his passions, and passed out exhausted right there on the spot.

DAMSEL. Aye, he does that.

BRIGANDESS. Understandably vexed and seeking satisfaction still, I relieved him of his ring, his sword and his horse. And left him there, panting – and pantless, of course.

DAMSEL. And did that give you the satisfaction you sought?

BRIGANDESS. Have you ridden the horse?

DAMSEL. I was going to wait till the wedding.

BRIGANDESS. So now ye know my terrible secret. And I

hope you're happy, having shamed me so. And in a public place. Where alcohol is served.

DAMSEL. But the horse is good, you say?

BRIGANDESS. O, what of that, when I am ruined?! For no sober man will have me now. 'Twere better you had killed me when you had the chance. In fact, here! *(tries to give her the sword)* Give it another go.

DAMSEL. There's no need of that. We have both been betrayed by a man. Regrettably, by the same man. Now we are two women alone in a world that measures a maiden more for what she has lost than what she brings to bear. Henceforward, we two shall be partners. Partners in crime! Why are you laughing? Stop that! What?

BRIGANDESS. You! A brigand!

DAMSEL. Aye, a brigand, I!

BRIGANDESS. But look at the way you're dressed.

DAMSEL. What's wrong with how I'm dressed?

BRIGANDESS. Not meaning to offend, but you jump out of a tree in that outfit, you'll catch wind in your knickers.

DAMSEL. I hadn't thought of that.

BRIGANDESS. There's more to being an outlaw than being good with a sword, and bad with the legal system. Ye must have survival skills.

DAMSEL. I'm fluent in Portuguese.

BRIGANDESS. So is the horse.

DAMSEL. And if you let me join you, you may keep the family sword.

BRIGANDESS. I've already *got* the sword.

DAMSEL. So you have. Hmm...

BRIGANDESS. Let's face it, lassie, I know you mean well, but ye don't bring much to the table. And anything I might have wanted from you, I already took from your man.

DAMSEL. Aye? Did he give you one of these?

(She grabs her and kisses her.)

BRIGANDESS. *(swooning)* My prince... *(realizing)* My God!

You kiss like him, too!

DAMSEL. Where do you think he learned it?

BRIGANDESS. My breath. My bosom. They catch and they heave. You are as skilled at pleasing a woman as any man living!

DAMSEL. And I don't get exhausted.

(She starts to kiss her again.)

BRIGANDESS. But I thought ye were a virgin.

DAMSEL. A virgin, yes. But I attended a four-year college.

(She gives the audience a sly wink, and kisses her again for good measure.)

FIN

GLADIATORS GLORIOUS

(A Roman arena. **GAIUS,** *a gladiator, laces up his boots.*
MAXIMUS, *another gladiator, joins him on the bench.)*

GAIUS. Morning, Max.

MAXIMUS. Morning, Gaius. They got you back on days again?

GAIUS. Yeah, they had me working C & L, but I needed the overtime.

MAXIMUS. Christians & Lions? What was that like?

GAIUS. Oh, you know, Christians, lions.

MAXIMUS. Sounds messy.

GAIUS. You know the old saying: the quicker the kill is, the slicker the spill is.

MAXIMUS. I don't know how those Christians do it.

GAIUS. They're scrappy some of 'em. I'll give 'em that.

MAXIMUS. But you're back here now?

GAIUS. Just through the holidays. Dayshift has the highest body count, so they had some openings.

MAXIMUS. Just doing my job.

GAIUS. Yeah, right, 'cause it's all you.

MAXIMUS. I do my share. I'm first-shift champion now, did you hear?

GAIUS. Yeah, and the new emperor's been stingy on the mercy.

MAXIMUS. There's a new emperor?

GAIUS. Oh, for the love of Cupid. The guy sits right across from you at work. You didn't notice he put on a little weight?

MAXIMUS. Only time I look to that end of the arena is when I'm waiting for the Thumb. As long as it's up, he could be Caligula for all I care.

GAIUS. He *is* Caligula!

MAXIMUS. Seriously? I never thought that guy'd get elected.

(Imperial fanfare.)

GAIUS. Here we go…

ANNOUNCER. HAIL CAESAR!

*(The **ANNOUNCER** is unintelligible, but we gather what's been said by the response of the gladiators.)*

GAIUS. *(standing)* Hail Caesar!

MAXIMUS. *(standing)* Yeah, what he said.

(They sit down again.)

GAIUS. So what's new with you?

MAXIMUS. Same old same old. I just got that big promotion. So now they got my name on the marquee outside.

GAIUS. Really?

MAXIMUS. That's what they tell me. I dunno. I can't read.

GAIUS. Did you get a bump?

MAXIMUS. Nah, it's nothin'. I ran into a door.

GAIUS. No, I mean a pay raise – They upped your take home, right?

MAXIMUS. I guess. But now I'm on salary, so it's longer hours. And they keep bringing in new blood to challenge me.

GAIUS. I guess they gotta keep it interesting.

MAXIMUS. Whatever. It's exhausting. Last Friday, I had to do three fights, a melee, a doubles match, and then another melee.

GAIUS. How'd you do?

MAXIMUS. Couple confirmed kills, one decap, but I almost lost a finger. Look at that nail.

GAIUS. Ouch. You better get that looked at.

MAXIMUS. Nah, it's just infected.

ANNOUNCER. THE CHAMPION! MAXIMUS MAXIMILLIUS PRIMUS!

MAXIMUS. Looks like I'm up.

GAIUS. Break a leg.

MAXIMUS. Don't tell me how to do my job.

GAIUS. Sorry.

(**MAXIMUS** *stands and waves to the crowd.*)

MAXIMUS. All right. Time to rip somebody a new one.

ANNOUNCER. THE CHALLENGER! GAIUS JULIUS NIHILUS!

(**GAIUS** *stands.*)

MAXIMUS. Whoops. I didn't mean that about the new one.

GAIUS. Nah, it's okay. Y'gotta talk trash. It's what separates us from the animals.

MAXIMUS. Who also work here.

GAIUS. *(offers to shake hands)* Best man?

MAXIMUS. Long as it's me.

ANNOUNCER. BATTLESPEARS! TWO MINUTES OR FIRST BLOOD.

(*They take up spears and fight.*)

GAIUS. Lotta new faces around here.

MAXIMUS. Yeah, well, I had a good month.

GAIUS. Is that Regulus?

MAXIMUS. What's left of him.

GAIUS. What happened?

MAXIMUS. Took a bludgeon to the privates. Hasn't been the same since. Beautiful singing voice, though.

(*They fight.* **MAXIMUS** *scores a superficial flesh wound.*)

GAIUS. Ouch! First blood. You got me. Good game.

(**MAXIMUS** *hits him again anyway.*)

Oof! Hey!

ANNOUNCER. TIME! FIRST BLOOD, MAXIMUS!

(*They stop fighting. The crowd cheers.*)

GAIUS. That was a cheap shot.

MAXIMUS. My bad. Won't happen again. Good game.

GAIUS. Thanks.

MAXIMUS. You got some new moves since the last time I saw you.

GAIUS. You ever try pulling a hungry lion off a tasty Christian?

(They sit.)

Hey, whatever happened to what's-her-name – little redhead used to work over on the women's side?

MAXIMUS. Alexandra?

GAIUS. She was a cutie.

MAXIMUS. Not my type.

GAIUS. I almost had a thing with her, y'know.

MAXIMUS. Seriously?

GAIUS. Yeah, we were working late one night. Decided to catch a bacchanal, after. Really hit it off. Turns out we killed the same guy, one time.

MAXIMUS. How'd you manage that?

GAIUS. Old friend of mine, Bibulus, you remember him?

MAXIMUS. I'm not good with names.

GAIUS. We were paired up for an axe-on-axe, and I cut off his arm.

MAXIMUS. That's gotta hurt.

GAIUS. So, of course, he gets the thumbs down. But he's a friend of mine, so I don't want to kill him outright – bad enough he's gonna blame me for the arm, right?

MAXIMUS. No kidding.

GAIUS. So I borrowed a gladius off one of the centurions – Did you know there's a way to run a guy through without hitting any vital organs?

MAXIMUS. First thing they teach you in Glad School.

GAIUS. So I stabbed him through. The crowd goes wild. And Bibulus lives to fight another day.

MAXIMUS. With no arm?

GAIUS. They fixed him up with an axe for a hand. Had him back in the arena the very next week.

MAXIMUS. What? Was he out of sick days?

GAIUS. We had that plague, remember?

MAXIMUS. Oh, right.

GAIUS. So he goes back to work, only now he's fighting left-handed. So Alexandra hacked off his other arm, and he bled to death in the first quarter. Didn't even make it to the Thumb.

ANNOUNCER. BY POPULAR ACCLAIM: MAXIMUS PRIMUS AND GAIUS NIHILUS!

(The crowd roars.)

MAXIMUS. Looks like they want a rematch.

GAIUS. So I haven't seen her around lately.

MAXIMUS. Who?

GAIUS. Alexandra.

MAXIMUS. Yeah, she's gone.

GAIUS. Transferred back to Athens?

MAXIMUS. No, I killed her.

GAIUS. What? Why?

MAXIMUS. She tried to mace me.

GAIUS. With a mace?

MAXIMUS. That's where I got this. *(points to his bump)* She said I was getting grabby.

GAIUS. So you were asking for it.

MAXIMUS. But I wanted to square things with her, so after the game, I follow her down to the locker room. Stabbed her in the back.

GAIUS. What?! Why'd you do that?!

MAXIMUS. Job security, buddy. You saw what she did to Bibulus. If I hadn't took her out when I did, she'd've killed half the guys in here, trust me.

ANNOUNCER. LEATHER AND FISTICUFFS! TWO MINUTES OR FIRST STRANGLEHOLD!

*(**MAXIMUS** picks up a leather strap.)*

MAXIMUS. Straps and scraps, you ready?

(**GAIUS** *decks him.*)

GAIUS. So you killed her?

(*They fight.*)

MAXIMUS. Hey, that's the job, buddy.

GAIUS. Fighting's the job. There's ways of not killing people.

MAXIMUS. Yeah, that sounds real exciting. What about the fans? This is a spectator sport, in case you forgot. That's why we let spectators in.

GAIUS. How many spectators were there in that locker room?

MAXIMUS. I'm just sayin' the plebs'd rather watch *me* slaughter a bunch of barbarians, than some Greek chick.

GAIUS. You could have disabled her. You didn't have to kill her.

MAXIMUS. Look, if it's any consolation, I didn't mean to. My hand slipped.

GAIUS. You slipped?! That's your excuse? What's wrong with you?! (*chokes him*)

MAXIMUS. Well, I'm having trouble breathing, at the moment.

ANNOUNCER. TIME!! STRANGLEHOLD NIHILUS!

(*They stop fighting.*)

MAXIMUS. Good fight. I think you might have me on points.

GAIUS. (*furious*) I *liked* her!

MAXIMUS. Little young for you.

GAIUS. That's right, she was eighteen! She had her whole life ahead of her. Brilliant career. Promising future. That's all gone now, thanks to you. All the things she'll never do. Places she'll never go. Never see Sparta. Never know the touch of a man.

MAXIMUS. She dumped you, didn't she?

GAIUS. We were taking a break!

MAXIMUS. Well, I wouldn't worry about Alexandra. She led a very full life.

GAIUS. What's that supposed to mean?

MAXIMUS. I'm just sayin' she didn't die without knowing the touch of a man.

GAIUS. How would you know that?

MAXIMUS. We hooked up, me and her.

GAIUS. When?

MAXIMUS. I dunno. Couple days after you left.

GAIUS. You and Alexandra?!

MAXIMUS. Yep.

GAIUS. And then you killed her?!

MAXIMUS. Don't act so surprised. Lotta ladies want a piece of this before they die.

GAIUS. Oh my gods! So you were her first!

MAXIMUS. Well, I was her last. Just between you and me, I don't think I was even close to coming in first. That girl was like a cat out of Hades – yowling and scratching – I never seen anything scream like that, and then get up and make breakfast.

ANNOUNCER. BATTLESWORDS! TWO MINUTES OR TO THE DEATH!

GAIUS. You… phallus!

MAXIMUS. Hey, that's uncalled for.

GAIUS. I'm gonna crucify you.

MAXIMUS. Now, calm down. Don't take it personal.

GAIUS. I'm going to personally eviscerate you.

MAXIMUS. Look, Guy, I had no idea she was your girl. If I knew you had a thing for her, I never would have told you about it, I swear.

GAIUS. Why do you think I asked for the transfer? Why do you think I spent my last three weeks here crying into my shield? Why do you think I came back here, during the busiest kill season, just to see if we still had a chance together??

MAXIMUS. Hey, take it easy! Gaius, I'm sorry!

GAIUS. You can tell Alexandra you're sorry – When you see her in Hades!

(*GAIUS goes for the kill.*)

ANNOUNCER. TIME! …TIME!!

MAXIMUS. Yes! Time! He said, time!

(*They stop fighting. MAXIMUS gets up off the ground.*)

Oh, thank gods! That was a close one. You scared the be-Jupiter outta me. Good game, buddy.

GAIUS. It's not over yet. (*saluting the emperor*) Hail Caesar!

MAXIMUS. Oh no… the Thumb.

GAIUS. (*forcing MAXIMUS to his knees*) Prepare to die.

(*They both look out across the arena.*)

ANNOUNCER. MAXIMUS MAXIMILLIUS PRIMUS, HAVING FAILED IN TWO OF THREE BOUTS… THE DECISION FALLS TO CAESAR!

GAIUS. Here it comes…

MAXIMUS. Thumbs up, thumbs up, thumbs up. Pluto, please, let it be thumbs up.

(*Beat.*)

ANNOUNCER. CAESAR IS MERCIFUL!

(*The crowd groans. Smattering of boos.*)

MAXIMUS. Yes! Yes!! Thank you, Caligula! (*to the ground*) Thank you, Pluto! (*to the crowd*) Thank you, Romans! I love you guys!!

(**MAXIMUS** *waves to the crowd.*)

Oh, wow. Whew! (*to GAIUS*) What a day, huh? Thank gods, that's over. I gotta tell you, Gaius, you really deserve this victory. You earned it. I mean that. (*offering to shake hands*) No hard feelings?

GAIUS. I think we're square.

(*GAIUS stabs him.*)

MAXIMUS. Oh… Ow.

GAIUS. Whoops. I slipped. My bad.

> (MAXIMUS *falls, dying.* GAIUS *gives the emperor a thumbs up.*)

> Sorry 'bout that, boss! Won't happen again! *(waving to the crowd)* Thank you, Romans! I love this job!

FIN

HARRIET HARLOWE:
THE HARLOT OF MARLOWE
IN
"THE HARLOT AND THE HIGHWAYMAN"

(A public road. A **YOUTHFUL HIGHWAYMAN** *kneels by the wayside, clasping a rosary.)*

NEWBERRY. Saints forgive me for what I am about to do. But what choice have I in it? There'll be heaven to pay if I do naught. Marry an' there will. *(hears a noise)* Someone is coming. Courage, man!

(He abruptly exits into the woods. Enter **HARRIET HARLOWE,** *the parish harlot.)*

HARRIET. *(singing)* Sweet Briony sailed a brothel ship
That moored just off the town,
And when she ran her bloomers up,
The seamen all ran down – What's this?

(Spotting the rosary on the ground, she stops singing, and draws her dagger.)

HARRIET. Who's there? Come out with ye!

*(***NEWBERRY*** enters, sword drawn and trembling.)*

NEWBERRY. There's no need to fear, lass.

HARRIET. Then why are ye trembling?

NEWBERRY. I mean that I mean you no peril.

HARRIET. Ye've a humourous way of showin' it, with a blade-point at me breast.

NEWBERRY. I want only your gold and whatever valuables you have about you.

HARRIET. And what if it's me heart that's golden? Will ye have that, too?

NEWBERRY. What – ? No, just your pocket coins'll do.

HARRIET. There's a shame for that's the least of me assets.

(She hands him her money pouch.)

NEWBERRY. Why? What else have ye?

(She draws a sword and attacks.)

HARRIET. Well, there's me fightin' spirit. Me sparklin' wit. Me bodice cut low for easy access. An' that's just a few o' me priceless commodities.

NEWBERRY. *(retreating)* I don't wish to harm you!

HARRIET. Now, there's news you should nae share with your victim.

NEWBERRY. I am warning you!

HARRIET. And I am taking it under advisement.

(She presses the attack and handily defeats him.)

NEWBERRY. Mercy, sweet angel, have mercy!

HARRIET. You call this highway robbery?? *(takes back her money)*

NEWBERRY. I confess I am new to the field. 'Tis only me first day.

HARRIET. Well, it takes a bit o' practice.

NEWBERRY. Will you kill me now?

HARRIET. Oh, there's no cause to cower. Get up.

NEWBERRY. No, I'm asking – Will you, please, kill me? 'Twould be a benevolence on me, for I've naught to live for. I have failed at every job I ever apprenticed – goldsmith, silversmith, locksmith, tinker.

HARRIET. You couldn't even tink?

NEWBERRY. And now I am a dismal cutpurse, to boot, for I could not mug a wee damsel.

HARRIET. Y'think I look wee in this outfit?

NEWBERRY. There is no hope for me!

HARRIET. Now, don't be so hard on yourself. You had no way of knowing you'd accosted a professional.

NEWBERRY. You? You are a professional highwayperson?

HARRIET. Uh... No.

NEWBERRY. A swordswoman?

HARRIET. No.

NEWBERRY. Hired blade? Mercenary? Pickpocket?

HARRIET. Let's just say I'm a professional, and leave it at that. The point is, I am no stranger to being accosted in the woods by strangers.

NEWBERRY. You've been waylaid before?

HARRIET. Before, aft, you name it.

NEWBERRY. Then you can show me how it's done!

HARRIET. Now why would a pious lad like yourself want to take up thieving?

NEWBERRY. 'Twas religion drove me to it, lass.

HARRIET. Ah! That old story.

NEWBERRY. I have fallen sinfully behind on me tithings of late.

HARRIET. The good Lord'll forgive it. Ye'll make it up to him next week.

NEWBERRY. Aye, but what if I am struck by lightning, in the meantime, and find myself roasting in a fiery pit for lack of a few timely pittance?

HARRIET. Sounds like you've been talking to Abbott Filcher.

NEWBERRY. Aye, he's a good and saintly man. Saved me from me own damnation with a Sabbath day loan.

HARRIET. That old shylock? He charges thruppence on the shilling.

NEWBERRY. And now I am into the Abbey for 3,000 thruppence. And the Abbot's henchmonks have sworn to break me legs, if I don't pay it prompt.

HARRIET. Aye, I know the monks well. And they are, indeed, hard on the legs.

NEWBERRY. Are you church-going yourself, lass?

HARRIET. Nae, it's mostly the church comes to me. *(glancing at her pocket watch)* Well, since it's for a good cause,

I suppose I can give you a few pointers, afore me next appointment.

NEWBERRY. Thank'ee, miss. Ye'll nae regret it.

HARRIET. Too late for that.

(She draws her sword. They spar.)

HARRIET. Now the first step, when you've got a coney cornered, is not to let her know you mean her no harm.

NEWBERRY. It is?

HARRIET. You *do* mean her harm.

NEWBERRY. I do?

HARRIET. In fact, if she's not careful, you may harm her just for the sport of it

NEWBERRY. 'S not very sporting.

HARRIET. You may harm her in ways she's never imagined!

NEWBERRY. Such as?

HARRIET. Use your imagination.

NEWBERRY. *(He does.)* Oh my! No, I would never – !

HARRIET. Yes, you would.

NEWBERRY. 'Tis nae polite.

HARRIET. That's sweet, lad, but it lacks desperation. A wild-eyed look and a disheveled mane will do more to strike fear in the heart of a man – *(tousles his hair)* – and strike a few other things in parts of a woman – than any amount of skill with a blade. *(pointedly)* Though bladework is also desirable.

NEWBERRY. *(He nods.)* Yes, ma'am.

HARRIET. A passion for the crime inspires confidence in one's robber.

NEWBERRY. I wouldn't want to disappoint my victims.

HARRIET. Will you have my money, then?

NEWBERRY. I will. I must! For I am at desperation's door. *And* on the brink o' madness!

HARRIET. Nice. And if I do not cooperate?

NEWBERRY. I will harm you in ways you can only fantasize about – I will pillage and plunder you. Demean, despoil and ruin you. I will strip you of your dignity, ravage your reputation, and desecrate the temple of your self-esteem! I will wrench your innocence from its socket and return it to you sullied and bent – if I return it at all – which I don't think I will, as I quite like it!

HARRIET. Well, uh…

NEWBERRY. Too much?

HARRIET. Close enough. Second, you must not be so timid with your blade. Bandy it about. Fit the buckle to your swash, as it were. Be aggressive.

NEWBERRY. Arr!

HARRIET. Be aggressive without letting your guard down.

NEWBERRY. Hurr!

HARRIET. That's better.

NEWBERRY. Is it?

HARRIET. Not really. Where's your vigor, lad? Do you want the Holy Virgin to get what's coming to her?

NEWBERRY. I do. I sincerely do.

HARRIET. Then have at me! You fight like ye're fighting a girl.

NEWBERRY. But I am.

HARRIET. But you are not. You are fighting a man.

(He fights harder.)

You are fighting a very large man.

(He fights even harder.)

A great ogre of a man.

(He bellows and charges at her.)

You are fightin' Abbot Filcher!

NEWBERRY. Die!!!

HARRIET. And all of his monks.

NEWBERRY. Yargh!!

(He disarms her.)

HARRIET. Now you have won.

NEWBERRY. I have, at that!

HARRIET. Now what?

NEWBERRY. Now you would give me your money, I think.

HARRIET. I think not.

NEWBERRY. No?

HARRIET. Now I would flee.

NEWBERRY. You're right! They've been doing that. But how am I to prevent it?

HARRIET. How indeed?

NEWBERRY. I should seize you.

HARRIET. Seize me, please. *(He does.)* Oo! Snug.

NEWBERRY. Now you are helpless in my arms.

HARRIET. So it seems. But now you must learn to fight dirty.

NEWBERRY. How dirty?

(She knees him in the groin.)

HARRIET. About like that.

(They fight dirty. After a struggle, he recaptures her.)

NEWBERRY. Aha!

HARRIET. *(melodramatically)* What, will you have your way with me?

NEWBERRY. What – No!

HARRIET. Yes.

NEWBERRY. I just want your gold.

HARRIET. No man wants only gold.

NEWBERRY. They don't?

HARRIET. I see the way you're eying my bodice.

NEWBERRY. It seems rude.

HARRIET. Well, yes, that's the appeal.

NEWBERRY. And the ladies like this?

HARRIET. Well, they have no choice, do they?

NEWBERRY. I suppose not.

HARRIET. Go on, then, rip it!

NEWBERRY. What?

HARRIET. My bodice, rip it!

NEWBERRY. But it's such a nice fabric.

HARRIET. Never mind, I'll do it. *(She rips her own bodice.)*

NEWBERRY. Milady!

(She grabs him and kisses him.)

NEWBERRY. Honestly, lass, I have no desire to despoil you.

HARRIET. Yes, you have!

NEWBERRY. You're right, I have!

HARRIET. You've waited your whole life for this moment.

NEWBERRY. Longer!

HARRIET. And ye'll let nothing stand in your way.

NEWBERRY. Nothing with feet!

(She slaps him.)

HARRIET. Inhuman brute! Will you savage my chastity? Here in this dark, lush, and picturesque forest. With what looks like a nice, soft pile of leaves over there.

NEWBERRY. Well, I hadn't planned –

HARRIET. Then you'd better improvise.

NEWBERRY. All right, I *will* have my way with you!

HARRIET. Yes!

NEWBERRY. But first the gold –

(He snatches her belt pouch.)

HARRIET. No! First the way!

(She snatches it back. They tussle briefly. She kisses him, then punches him.)

NEWBERRY. Ow!

HARRIET. And that's just a taste of what's in store for you, if you dare to lay a finger on me!

NEWBERRY. *(thinks about it)* Well, my fingers *could* use the exercise.

(He undresses, turning his back politely, so that she can

do the same. She doesn't.)

NEWBERRY. Do not think to flee, while my back is turned, for I will surely follow you to the ends of the earth, and when I find you, I shall have my way with you there. And it will be cold there. So it's best to stay and do it here, where there's leaves.

(Meanwhile, she is about to make off with his belt pouch and his sword.)

HARRIET. And speaking of leaves, it is time I took mine.

NEWBERRY. What – where are you going?

HARRIET. I'm sorry, lad, but I have business in the town. And you know the monks don't like to wait.

NEWBERRY. But I am learning so much.

HARRIET. And I am learning naught. And earning less. So I must go, and I'll have your gold for me troubles.

NEWBERRY. What about my troubles?

HARRIET. Yours seem quite beyond resolution. *(exiting)* Remember what I have taught you, and there'll be a monk along in half an hour to try it out on. Oh, who am I kidding? He'll be along in six minutes.

NEWBERRY. Will you leave me thus unsatisfied?

HARRIET. Not to worry, lad – *(kisses him)* – I'm sure I'll be back.

NEWBERRY. *(blocks her path)* No! I will not let you abandon me so.

HARRIET. You forget, you are overmatched. *(draws her sword)* And underarmed.

NEWBERRY. You forget, I am desperate.

(He charges her and wrestles a weapon away from her. They fight in earnest now.)

HARRIET. You are a quick study. I'll give you that.

NEWBERRY. You'll give me more than that, wench!

HARRIET. I like your spark. A few cinders more, an' you're like to have a fire.

NEWBERRY. I want what's rightfully mine!

HARRIET. I thought you wanted the gold.

NEWBERRY. And the gold!

(He disarms her. She slaps him. He kisses her.)

HARRIET. Villain!

(She slaps him again. He slaps her. She kisses him.)

NEWBERRY. Harlot!

(They roll around on the ground, alternately fighting, kissing, wrestling, kissing and fighting again.)

HARRIET. Libertine!

NEWBERRY. Bedswindler!

HARRIET. Hooligan!

NEWBERRY. Witch!

HARRIET. Craven potmender!

NEWBERRY. Brazen call damsel!

HARRIET. Insufferable –

NEWBERRY. Curvaceous –

HARRIET. Incompetent –

NEWBERRY. Shameless –

HARRIET. Maurading, lascivious, criminal Adonis!

NEWBERRY. Ravishing, strumpeted, ruby-lipped vixen!

HARRIET. I love it when you talk bawdy. *(She throws herself into his arms.)* You are victorious.

NEWBERRY. I am Neville. Victorious is my horse.

HARRIET. I am Harriet.

NEWBERRY. Harriet Harlowe? The parish harlot?

HARRIET. You've heard of me?

NEWBERRY. You run a bawdy parlour in Devon Street that rents by the hour for seven pounds three.

HARRIET. Does it bother you, that I earn my keep the old fashioned way?

NEWBERRY. Why, it's the best news I've had all day! *(turns to go)*

HARRIET. Where are you going?

NEWBERRY. It occurs to me there's an unsuspecting monk in Devon Street, who's going to be very surprised to see me. And if I get there before you do, he'll still have a pocketful of pound notes!

HARRIET. Will you leave me thus unsatisfied?

NEWBERRY. Not to worry, my sweet. *(takes her in his arms and kisses her again)* I'm sure you'll be back.

(He drops her and bounds off into the forest.)

HARRIET. Oh!!

FIN

JOLLY JACK JUNIOR:
THE BUCCANEER'S BAIRN

(The deck of a sailing ship. Sounds of a sea battle raging – cannonfire and sabers clashing – pirates boarding the ship. **PIRATE WILLY** *bounds onto the stage, a cutlass in either hand.)*

WILLY. Avast, ye brigands! Yo ho! Strike colors and submit to be boarded. *(calling to his crew)* Haul aft to the main-helm, me hearties. Hoist the mizzenpoop and trim fast the doozy. Take no prisoners, save the women and agile boys. And a lubbard's blarney to the bloke who brings me the brigands' captain. Harrr! *

WENCH. *(offstage)* Unhand me, ye scurvy scuttlefish!

WILLY. Man that woman, mate, she's gettin' away! Mind your starboard jowl! No, your starboard!

(A resounding SMACK from offstage. **WILLY** *winces. A* **PIRATE WENCH** *rushes in and tries to get past him, but he sheaths his blades and catches her in one arm.)*

WILLY. Hold there, sea wench! Where ye think yer garn?

WENCH. To hell's britches ere I answer to the likes of you, ye daft cutlet. This be a pirate vessel ye've boarded. We're all pirates here!

WILLY. Aye, and it's pirates I'm pillaging today – the devil take 'em – for I am One-Eyed Willy, the buccaneer's bane. Have ye not heard o' me?

WENCH. Nay, I think I'd remember that.

WILLY. Well, I'm new. *(then with gusto)* Orphaned by pirates I was! And I mean to have me revenge on every last scoundrel. Now take me to your captain 'fore I do something I might not regret.

---

*Author's Note: Some of these words are made up.

WENCH. What, will you have your pleasures with me unwilling corpse, ye filthy, whoreson, motherless son of a sea cow?

WILLY. Motherless I be – for orphaned by pirates I was – but I'd sooner suckle a manatee's teat than mingle my bilges with the likes of you, ya withered old crone. Why, you must be nearly 28, by the looks of ye.

WENCH. I don't look a day over 25, an' you know it, ye scurrilous scallywag. And I may be withered – by contemporary standards – but I'm still as fine a piece of sea bass as you'll never lay fingers on. Now unfist me before I pluck out your other eye, ye couthless bootblack.

WILLY. Nay, and ye'll nae touch me eye, till I've seen your captain with it. Now where be the brigand?

WENCH. What would the likes of you want with the likes of Captain Jack?

WILLY. Captain Jack? Did you say Captain Jack??

WENCH. Aye, Captain Jack, the Terror and Scourge of the High Seas, and some of the low ones, too. What's the matter, mate? Ye look weak in the gills at the very sound of the name. And rightly so, for there's no more treacherous pirate on land or sea. Or up in space, for that matter. Ye've good reason to be terrified.

WILLY. Terrified? I don't know the meaning of the word!

WENCH. It means scared.

WILLY. I know what it means! I was being facetious.

WENCH. I don't know the meaning of the word!

(He rolls his good eye at her, but goes on.)

WILLY. Fear is for cowards, says I. And I'll have none of it!

WENCH. Then why do ye tremble in yer galoshes at the mere mention of Captain Jack? *(He flinches at the mention. So she does it again.)* Cap'n Jack! Cap'n Jack!

WILLY. Shut your fish hole, ye briny deck trollop! I'm not afeared o' your Captain Jack.

WENCH. Ha! So yer a coward and a liar, to boot!

WILLY. Nae, but I tell ye true, sea slut, it pangs me to hear the name, because I've sought this Captain Jack for near me entire life. Since I was naught but a wee bairn in me swaddles growin' up in a lubbard's orphanage north of New Norfolk, I prayed myself to sleep at night cursing the name of Cap'n Jack, the pirate that orphaned me. I'd lie abed awake in that unholy monastery with nothing but me simmering hatred and the love o' God to feed me when the wretched nuns would not. No sooner was I old enough to be out of me diapers, than I set off in quest of me quarry. I searched the world over, far and wide, o'er hill and mountain, desert and near-desert. And then I figured out Captain Jack was a pirate name, and I started searching the seas.

WENCH. You poor wastling. And how long have you been questing?

WILLY. Nigh on three weeks.

WENCH. Three weeks out of diapers?! How do you bear it?

WILLY. Double thick breeches, lass. Double thick breeches.

WENCH. But what's so all-bloody important about catchin' Captain Jack?

WILLY. I just told ye, didn't I?! Have ye not paid a heed of a word I have said?

WENCH. Not really. I was admirin' yer pectorals.

WILLY. Well, what does any orphan rogue of a waif search high and low the world over for – journeying near and far, far and wide – driving himself half mad with grief, and the other half with rum?

WENCH. Well, it sounds like the love of a fine wench is what you're describing, if I know me obsessions. That, or a whale.

WILLY. *(bitter laugh)* Aye, a wench, you might say. But not a fine one, by any means. Y'see, it was Captain Jack who left me a motherless orphan in that godless orphanage.

WENCH. You mean…?

WILLY. That's right. Captain Jack – your own Captain Jack – is me mother.

WENCH. Your mother?

WILLY. That's right.

WENCH. Captain Jack?

WILLY. That's right.

WENCH. Is your mother?!

WILLY. Aye, you heard me the first three times. Captain Cecily Jack, the Scourge of the Seas, the captain of this vessel. The Demon Queen of the Oceans Green. She's my mother, an I'll have you know. Now will you take me to her, or do I have to keelhaul it out of you?

WENCH. Stow your threats, for I'll tell ye right now. *I'm* the captain of this vessel!

(She grabs a cutlass out of his scabbard and takes a swing at him. He barely ducks and draws his other blade. They fight.)

WILLY. You! Y'are my mother? Can it be? After all these years of praying – and weeks of actually looking – I've finally found you.

WENCH. Save your wind for other sails, boy, for I am no man's mother I.

WILLY. Aye?

WENCH. Aye!

WILLY. Y'are a liar then! For the whole sea-faring world knows the legend of the she-pirate Cecily Jack, captain of the Boatswain's Booty and how, not fifteen years agone, she took to her cabins in the midst of a storm, complaining of cramps and bloated with "sea-weight." There, she secretly gave birth to a strapping baby boy, who – fearful for her standing in the naval profession – she wrapped in an old galley cloth, and heaved him over the stern into the storm.

WENCH. Not much of a secret, then, was it?

WILLY. I stand before you today, that same strapping boy become a strapping man. An' that's the God's truth.

WENCH. Then God's a damn liar! For if your story were true, you'd barely be fifteen years old.

WILLY. Aye, but a strapping fifteen. I mentioned I was strapping, didn't I?

WENCH. Well, I can see that for myself.

WILLY. It runs in the family. Captain Cecily Jack, it's said, was but a slip of a wee lass of thirteen when she took on a whole boatload of pirates single-handed. They made her their captain that very day, out of respect for her cunning.

WENCH. They do love my cunning.

(She deftly disarms him and shoves her blade under his chin.)

WENCH. Now, have ye any last words before Momma tucks you in… *to Davey Jones' locker!?*

WILLY. Ye'd be so callous to off your own offspring?

WENCH. For callin' me an old crone? I'd slit my own throat, if I caught me doing it.

WILLY. Yer heart is not wrenched for sorrow by the harrowsome tale of me parentless past?

WENCH. Like ye said yourself, sailor, the whole whalin' world knows the terrible tale of the tot I tossed in the torrents, that stormy night, those many years agone. And not a week goes by but you and every other mongrel pup in Poseidon's Christendom comes lookin' for me, claimin' to be my longlost, hopin' to snuggle a motherly hug and a day's rate of rations out of me for pity. But the day's not half done, 'fore they're all clapped in irons and fed to the sharks, because not one of 'em thought to mention the *golden locket* I tucked into the seam of the wee squalling newborn's bedding – so that one day his doting mother would know him on sight – before I dumped him off the poop deck and into the squalls.

(She prepares to kill him.)

WILLY. I have a locket.

WENCH. Ye what?

WILLY. Aye, a golden locket that was lodged in me gullet when they dredged me out of the foam at New Norfolk. They had to uncork it from me ere I could breathe right. I didn't know what it was for, but the sisters at the orphanage let me keep it because it was too sticky with sea goo to pawn at the rectory shop.

WENCH. Then it's true! Ye are my wee castaway bairn!

WILLY. As sure as ye're my bairn-casting mairn.

WENCH. And you've come all this way to be reunited with your prodigal mum?

WILLY. Aye, mother, I have.

WENCH. I hope yer not thinkin' we can just take up where we left off.

WILLY. Well, we left off with you heaving me to the sharks, so, no, I'd rather not start there.

WENCH. I guess that's understandable.

WILLY. Nor would I care to start any otherwhere, for I want nothing to do with you.

WENCH. What? Then why'd ye come all this way?

WILLY. To gut you like a salmon fish, ye heartless harpy!

(He knocks her backward and seizes her weapon. They fight.)

WILLY. I've hated you all these many years, for abandoning me when I was but a hapless swaddle, and I mean to fillet you alive for it and see if that improves me self-image.

WENCH. Have ye no mercy then?

WILLY. Mercy? Why, ye're lucky I don't lash you to the mainmast and flog out a drubbing for every time the cruel sisters of Saint Salome's wore out a leather strap on my behind – *(sobs)* – when it should have been me own mum!

(He stops fighting and starts to weep, then lunges at her – pinning her to the mast.)

WILLY. Have you naught to say for yourself, before I scuttle you like an old harbor tug?

WENCH. You'd murder your own mother?

WILLY. With no more remorse than I'd throttle a mangy wharf rat.

WENCH. Well, all right, then, do it and be quick about it.

WILLY. I'll do it when I please.

WENCH. You'll do it when I say, I haven't got all day for this.

WILLY. Don't tell me what to do.

WENCH. I'll tell you anything I like. This is still my ship.

WILLY. Ye're not the boss o' me!

WENCH. Don't sass your mother! It's insubordination.

WILLY. I don't care if y'are my mother. I'll sass as I please. And I'll kill you when I kill you and not a moment before. For what you've done to me, I ought to kill my grandmother, too.

WENCH. Oh, leave her be, son. The woman has cats.

WILLY. All right, my father then. I'll kill him. Where is he?

WENCH. Sweet Neptune's privy! If I knew that, you think I'd still be running a boat? It's every little girl's dream – even a successful career pirate like myself – to give up all her ambitions and raise a child in a little house with a white picket fence and a dumbfounded hulk of a man at her side to take care of her, just like in all the romance tales.

WILLY. Really?

WENCH. No, of course not.

WILLY. Then tell me who my father is. Or so help me, I'll spit you where you stand.

WENCH. You'd best go ahead and spit me then, for I haven't the slightest idea. It could be any one of these black-guards. *(She gestures toward the crew.)*

WILLY. You mean to say ye slept with your entire crew?

WENCH. Once a week, whether they needed it or not.

There's not a man jack on Cap'n Jack's boat hasn't had Cap'n Jack's booty. Promotes morale. There's no greater loyalty than the love of a man for the only woman who'll have him. Why do you think they made me captain?

WILLY. I thought it was because you took on a boatload of pirates single-handed.

WENCH. Aye. But I didn't use my hands.

WILLY. Ugh! You're nothing but a dirty deck harlot! A galley slattern! A cargo ho!

WENCH. Watch your mouth. I'm still your mother.

WILLY. I'd rather I were still a motherless bastard than the whoreson whelp of a scullery pump.

WENCH. It's what I had to be, son, in order to survive. The sea is a cruel mistress. And she's even crueler if you're a supple, young lass on a ship full of men whose only other mistress is the cruel sea. It was either learn to love my crew, or learn to love being tied down to a galley table while my crew learned to love me. And let me tell you, they're slow learners. So I made my choices. Choices you, as a man, may never have to make.

WILLY. You forget, I was raised in a catholic orphanage.

WENCH. Oh, that's right.

WILLY. Why do you think they call me One-Eyed Willy?

WENCH. It's not because of the patch?

WILLY. No, the patch is so no one asks me why the nuns keep callin' me One-Eyed Willy.

WENCH. Ew.

WILLY. But we don't have to talk about that.

(He straightens his eyepatch.)

WENCH. Am I proud of what I've done? Am I proud of tossing my only babe in a bundle off the poop deck in a storm to spare him from a life of piracy which it turns out he went ahead and took up on his own anyway? …Frankly, no, that's kind of embarrassing. But am I proud of being able to suck a cannonball through forty feet of cast iron stove pipe? Hell, yes, I am! You try it. It's quite an accomplishment. But this is the life that chose me, son. And there's nothing for it, but to make the best chowder from what's in your net.

WILLY. I never thought of it that way. I guess I didn't know.

WENCH. There's a lot of things you didn't know about me, lad.

WILLY. But I want to know! I want us to be a family. A pirate family.

WENCH. That's all I needed to hear. Come to me arms, me brackish boy.

(They embrace. They kiss. It lasts a little too long. He suddenly pulls away.)

WILLY. Ugh! Mum! I'm your boy!

WENCH. I warned you I was a fine dish of sea bass.

WILLY. You are, at that.

WENCH. I told ye.

WILLY. And how was I?

WENCH. You kiss like a shipful of sailors on shore leave.

WILLY. And that's good?

WENCH. No, that's very bad.

WILLY. Arr!

WENCH. But you'll learn...

(She puts her arm around him, and they wander off into the salty sunset...)

WILLY. So how'd you come to find yourself alone at thirteen on a boat full of pirates in the first place?

WENCH. They answered my ad.

FIN

MAIDS MADE MEN

(A secluded wood. Enter a **DISTRAUGHT MADEMOI-SELLE**, *bearing a pair of pants.)*

ANTOINETTE. O, what have I done? Spurned the unwanted advances of my fencing master – That's what I've done! Stolen his pants and fled into the forest – What was I thinking?

But it was the only way to prevent him pursuing me into the brambles and overcoming my initial resistance there in the prickly thicket, with his manful wiles.

O, why did I not suppress my maiden umbrage and succumb to his unsubtle seductions? How will I show my face again in the village where I was born and raised, after Monsieur Latoit returns and blackens my name there?

My mother will never forgive me for forsaking such a promising match. The second most eligible swordsman in the province? And headmaster of the prestigious local academy for damsels! Now I shall never gain admission to those hallowed halls where so many maids are made women.

I have no choice but to leave the village and the only life I've ever known, for I can never go back there. Yet, neither can I go forward, to the next village and a new life, as it is unsafe and unseemly for a young and supple woman alone and unescorted to travel these woods at night. Or on weekends.

Especially a virgin who wishes to retain what remains of her honour. For there are rumoured to be thieves and rapscallions about – rude ruffians with workman's hands, and playman's morals – who would think nothing of having their way with me, and with my honour.

No! I must not dwell upon the unthinkable fate that awaits me, within these shadowy and illicit woods, teeming with rugged, handsome highwaymen, lurking behind every tree. Eying me with prying eyes, and soon-to-be-prying fingers.

O, would that I had been born a man and free to flee my checked past – and these checkered pants – and travel through the woods alone and unescorted – like a man – to a new life that awaits me in the next village, or the village after that. Or possibly even the third village over, which I hear has a very fashionable shopping district.

But wait! That's it!! I still have Monsieur Latoit's pants. And his sword. And I guess this is his shirt. (Oh, I hope he's not cold.) I need only don these convincing vestments, and assume a certain masculine swagger, and no one alive – at least no one living in this repressed and bygone era – would suspect that I am not what I appear to be: A non-woman! Which is to say, a man! *(brandishing the sword)* And a dashing swashbuckler of a man, at that! And no man, dashing or otherwise, would dare to trifle with me! *(sighs)* Though I will miss the trifling, now I think on't.

But hark! My feminine intuition tells me that someone is coming! I must hide and disguise me.

(She exits into the woods, just as RENÉ, *a female highwayman-in-men's-clothing, bursts in, with sword drawn, and a moustache drawn on.)*

RENÉ. Stand fast! Who's there! En garde! *(Looks around perplexed. There's no one there.)* Hmm. That's strange. I thought I heard voices. Lady voices. A ghost, perhaps? But, more likely, it is the specter of my own girlish guilt that haunts me. Guilt over a past so shameful that I dare not speak of it, except when I am alone in a secluded wood, musing to myself, as I am now.

For it was not so long ago that I was lured into this very forest by a lecherous fencing master, and forced to flee from his clutches, and from my former life, in his clothes, to lead the life of a notorious highwayman.

For, despite all outward appearances, I am neither notorious. Nor a man. (Nor is this much of a highway. They really ought to fix this place up.) But a woman!

(Rips open her shirt. She is wearing a frilly brassiere or camisole.)

A lusty, buxom, young woman, forced to live as a man for my own survival – and as a professional courtesy to the other highwaymen, who consider a woman in the woods to be almost as unlucky as an albatross on a ship. Which really makes me wonder what they do on those ships.

(suddenly distraught) O, the shame of it! ...No! I must not weep! Back, tears! I must not show myself to be less than manly, in these parts. For if I am caught here in this wood – a woman alone and distraught – the fate that could befall me would be far worse than any fate I have ever imagined, or dreamed. Or read about in romantic novellas.

(Sound of footsteps in the underbrush.)

Someone is coming! They cannot see me like this!

*(**ANTOINETTE** bursts in, in Latoit's outfit, with sword drawn, and a moustache drawn on.)*

ANTOINETTE. Halt! Who goes there?

RENÉ. *(rebuttoning herself)* I was not crying!

ANTOINETTE. Who are you? What are you doing in these woods?

RENÉ. I could ask you the same question.

ANTOINETTE. Touché! *(then)* En garde! *(attacks)*

(They fight.)

And if you are not crying, then why do tears bestreak your makeup?

RENÉ. It's not makeup! These woods are very dusty.

ANTOINETTE. *(unconvinced)* Uh huh…

RENÉ. And if you must know, I stumbled in the underbrush, and a tree branch struck me in my manhood. *(grimly)* But I would not expect a woman to understand.

ANTOINETTE. Who are you calling a woman?

RENÉ. *(confused)* Who do you *think* I'm calling a woman?

ANTOINETTE. I am wearing *trousers!*

RENÉ. Hmm… So you are. That is odd.

ANTOINETTE. What woman wears trousers in the woods?

RENÉ. *(glancing down at her own trousers)* None, I guess.

ANTOINETTE. With these shoes?

RENÉ. You're right, you're right.

ANTOINETTE. Especially itchy trousers. Sticky with brambles. I shall never get them clean.

RENÉ. So you are… a man?

ANTOINETTE. Yes, I am. And a highwayman, at that. Now hand over your gold before I give your manhood something to really cry about.

RENÉ. If you are a man, what are you doing in the woods alone?

ANTOINETTE. Whatever we men do alone in the woods, of course.

RENÉ. I see. And what is that?

ANTOINETTE. Oh, you know. Man stuff.

RENÉ. Such as?

ANTOINETTE. Well, you know, the usual sort of thing. Traveling about. Unescorted.

RENÉ. Uh huh…

ANTOINETTE. Spitting and passing wind without excusing oneself. That sort of thing.

RENÉ. Oh, for the love of St. Peter!

ANTOINETTE. What?

RENÉ. You don't know the first thing about pretending to be a man.

ANTOINETTE. *(curious)* Why? What's the first thing?

RENÉ. You don't even have the voice right!

ANTOINETTE. *(deeper)* Why? What's the first thing?

RENÉ. And you've been crying, too.

ANTOINETTE. Have not!

RENÉ. Then why do tears streak your makeup?

ANTOINETTE. Perhaps I also sat on a tree branch.

RENÉ. No, no! The tree branch *hits* you.

ANTOINETTE. I don't get it.

RENÉ. You are an embarrassment to women-disguised-as-men everywhere.

ANTOINETTE. I am not! And I'm not a woman! And how would you know what embarrasses us? Them!

RENÉ. Well, I am no authority on the subject, of course.

ANTOINETTE. Of course not! Nor am I.

RENÉ. But just look at you! You are far too pretty for this.

ANTOINETTE. *(offended)* Oh!! Were I a man, I should take offence at your emasculating flattery. Which I am. And I do. And thank you so much.

RENÉ. You are hopeless.

ANTOINETTE. Must I prove my mettle?

RENÉ. No, never mind. I believe you. Now stand aside, I must be on my way.

ANTOINETTE. Not so fast. You must stand aside and let me be on my way. Or do you take me for less of a man than you?

RENÉ. No, about the same, actually.

ANTOINETTE. Good! Then get out of my way and let me pass. And hand over your gold. And stand aside. And who does your hair?

RENÉ. Well, which is it?

ANTOINETTE. Are you calling me indecisive?

RENÉ. Oh boy…

ANTOINETTE. Just for that, I shall have your gold *and* your shirt.

RENÉ. My shirt???

ANTOINETTE. This one makes me look fat. *(reaches for René's shirt buttons)*

RENÉ. Impudent girl! Now you go too far!

ANTOINETTE. Boy!!

RENÉ. Who are you calling "boy"?

ANTOINETTE. *Me!* I'm a boy.

RENÉ. Oh, sorry. I thought it was an insult.

ANTOINETTE. *(realizing)* You're right, it *is* an insult. I am no boy, but a man!

RENÉ. You are no man, but a girl!

ANTOINETTE. I am no girl, but a woman. Or, no, a man! No, a pirate!

RENÉ. You are no pirate! Now stand aside or you will face my wrath.

ANTOINETTE. Not if you face mine first! *(lunging)* En garde!

RENÉ. *(beating her back)* No!

ANTOINETTE. *(lunging again)* En garde, I say!

RENÉ. Don't make me hurt you.

ANTOINETTE. Have at you!

RENÉ. Have at *you.*

ANTOINETTE. Take that!

RENÉ. *You* take it!

    (They fight.)

You fight well, for a woman, I'll give you that.

ANTOINETTE. That is because I apprenticed under the second finest swordsman in the province.

RENÉ. And you are not a woman.

ANTOINETTE. And I am not a woman!!

    (They fight.)

RENÉ. So you studied with Monsieur Latoit?

ANTOINETTE. Yes, you know him?

RENÉ. Why, yes, in fact, I myself – *(catches herself)* – know him.

    (They fight.)

RENÉ. So he taught you that maneuver?

ANTOINETTE. Yes.

RENÉ. And that?

ANTOINETTE. Yes! And this! And this! And this! And this one is called the Latoit Defense:

(*ANTOINETTE answers RENÉ's next lunge with a deft flurry of defensive maneuvers, which backs RENÉ across the clearing, disarms her, pins her against a tree, and in the same motion, plants a big kiss on her. They both look startled.*)

ANTOINETTE. Oh. Sorry. Still working on that one.

RENÉ. I see Monsieur Latoit is still up to his old tricks.

ANTOINETTE. What do you mean by that?

(*RENÉ fights back.*)

RENÉ. If I am not mistaken, Monsieur Latoit is still the headmaster of the prestigious local academy for damsels…

ANTOINETTE. Yes, he – ! *(then, realizing her mistake)* Oh –

RENÉ. He teaches only girls…

ANTOINETTE. Well, in general, perhaps –

RENÉ. And if you are one of his students…

ANTOINETTE. I really should be going.

RENÉ. Then, you, sir, are a girl!

(*ANTOINETTE suddenly throws down her weapon and collapses in tears.*)

ANTOINETTE. O, it's no use! I am living a lie! And have been for the last several minutes. For I am no highwayman, but a woman. Forced to resort to gentlemen's drawers to cloak my shame, and preserve my honour in these woods. And now that you know my secret you will surely have your way with me.

RENÉ. Thank you, no.

ANTOINETTE. Well, if you must ravage me, do it and be quick about it – but not too quick. Be a gentleman about it – but not too gentle. Rough – but not too rough – but almost too rough. More rough than gentle, really

RENÉ. That won't be necessary.

ANTOINETTE. No, it's all right. 'Tis no more than my fate. A fate that I have looked forward to with dread for most of the afternoon. And with anticipation. But mostly dread. But a little anticipation.

RENÉ. Kind of you to offer, but –

ANTOINETTE. Do as you will with me! Only promise me this: That once your will has been done, and your satisfaction taken, you will take me away from this place and the shame of it. And the shame of what we will do here.

RENÉ. I'm not going to do anything.

ANTOINETTE. Why not? Am I not beautiful?

RENÉ. Yes, yes. You're very pretty.

ANTOINETTE. I said "beautiful"!

RENÉ. Look…

ANTOINETTE. I *do* look fat!

RENÉ. I have to go.

ANTOINETTE. *(blocking her exit)* Don't you love me?

RENÉ. I only just met you.

ANTOINETTE. But surely you were attracted at first sight. That's how it works.

RENÉ. Honestly, you're a bit manly for my tastes.

ANTOINETTE. Manly, am I? I'll show you manly! *(She attacks.)*

RENÉ. Please! I've seen enough manly for one day!

ANTOINETTE. Have at you!

RENÉ. You're taking this the wrong way.

ANTOINETTE. What kind of man are you that would leave a damsel undefended in the woods?

RENÉ. A very bad man.

ANTOINETTE. That's what I like to hear!

RENÉ. No, but I'm good, too. With a bit of bad mixed in. I'm nice.

ANTOINETTE. Nice?! Ugh! You sound positively boring.

(stops fighting) All right, you can go.

RENÉ. Thank you.

ANTOINETTE. But answer me one thing –

RENÉ. Certainly.

ANTOINETTE. How is it that *you* know Monsieur Latoit?

RENÉ. *(caught)* Oh, um. Social circles, mostly.

ANTOINETTE. But that's impossible! The old fellow never gets out. I mean, look at these trousers. He rarely leaves the grounds of the academy, except when he is taking students into the woods for private instruction – *(gasps)*

RENÉ. It's not what you think!

ANTOINETTE. Then how did you know he'd been "up to his old tricks"?

RENÉ. Lucky guess.

ANTOINETTE. And why does your bosom heave with distress?

RENÉ. I told you, I took a tree branch.

ANTOINETTE. And who taught you the Latoit Defense?

RENÉ. Nobody. I don't know it. You brought it up.

ANTOINETTE. Then how do you explain *this*!

(She lunges. RENÉ instinctively defends, and in the same flurry of deft swordsmanship, ANTOINETTE ends up pinned to a tree as RENÉ plants a kiss on her.)

RENÉ. Oops. That just slipped out.

ANTOINETTE. It's you!

RENÉ. No, it's not!

ANTOINETTE. You're the girl that never came back! The one that got away!

RENÉ. No, I –

(ANTOINETTE suddenly rips open RENÉ's shirt, revealing her frilly underthings.)

ANTOINETTE. It *is* you!

RENÉ. O, it's true! O, the shame of it – !! *(realizes)* Wait, you've heard of me?

ANTOINETTE. The damsels at the academy talk about you all the time. We thought you'd run away and been mauled by bears. Or highwaymen. But look at you: You've become a notorious highwayperson yourself!

RENÉ. Why, thank you.

ANTOINETTE. You must come back to the academy. It would be such an inspiration to the other girls.

RENÉ. Really?

ANTOINETTE. You could even teach there!

RENÉ. Have you forgot Latoit? The headmaster will never let either of us on the grounds.

ANTOINETTE. Oh, I wouldn't worry about that old lecher. He may be the second finest swordsman in the province. But between the two of us – *(draws her sword)* – I think we're wearing the pants now.

(They stride off into the woods together.)

FIN

SIR SIMON'S SECOND

(A dueling ground. **TWO GENTLMEN** *meet to arrange a quarrel.)*

MANFRED'S MAN. Are you Sir Simon's second?

SIMON'S SECOND. So I am. And you? Sir Manfred's man?

MANFRED'S MAN. In a manner of speaking. Shall we proceed to the particulars?

SIMON'S SECOND. Of what?

MANFRED'S MAN. The duel, of course. Choice of weapons. Terms of surrender.

SIMON'S SECOND. Should not we await the arrival of the duelists?

MANFRED'S MAN. Oh, no, sir. That is what we seconds are for – to lay the groundwork, choose the ground, agree upon terms, time, terrain, and a florist – that our masters may take the field of honour, unpreoccupied with the minutiae of their mutual mutilation. Shall we say rapiers?

SIMON'S SECOND. I hope to think it would not come to that.

MANFRED'S MAN. I would not think to hope so. The offence the one has done the other – and the other duly returned – is such an injurious hurt that naught but violence may emend it.

SIMON'S SECOND. Suppose Sir Simon tendered his apology? Or I could tender one on his behalf.

MANFRED'S MAN. O, do not so, sir. That would surely shame him. It is a grave disservice to be so courteous.

SIMON'S SECOND. May we not be civil?

MANFRED'S MAN. Civility, of course, but not remorse. We must respect their disrespect.

SIMON'S SECOND. I do apologize, I meant nothing by it. Or did I?

MANFRED'S MAN. I take it this is your first time seconding?

SIMON'S SECOND. Indeed it is. My maiden melee, if you will.

MANFRED'S MAN. Then you should know that your master and mine have so affronted one another – over some no doubt insignificant and insipid slight – that there is no conceivable relief of their grievances, save to do one another some grievous harm. They have agreed to fight, and we, their seconds, to arrange the particulars of the proceeding, aid and abet their every need and provision, and attend to the least detail. Even going so far as to take the field of honour ourselves, in their steads, should either man falter or fail to appear.

SIMON'S SECOND. Oh, I see. Well, this is awkward.

MANFRED'S MAN. What is the matter, sir? You look positively ill.

SIMON'S SECOND. Only insofar as I am positive that Sir Simon is. He was feeling feverish at breakfast this morning, and sent me here with his regrets that he could not, in good conscience, subject Sir Manfred and yourself to whatever sudden influenza he's contracted.

MANFRED'S MAN. The "Dueler's Croup". I know the symptoms well. *(offering a pair of rapiers)* It seems the choice of weapons, then, is yours. I fear your first time seconding may be your last.

SIMON'S SECOND. I do not fret for that, for your man Manfred and I were classmates at Eton, and often sparred. I'm sure I should make short work of him in any earnest engagement.

MANFRED'S MAN. Then what is it that troubles you?

SIMON'S SECOND. Why, Manfred and myself share an alma mater, and therefore a lifelong bond of acquaintanceship. We are very nearly very dear friends. In fact, I offered to second Sir Simon, only in hopes of dissuading the two from furtherance of this vile business.

MANFRED'S MAN. Vile, is it? Have a care, sir. There are those who make it their business to be so vile.

SIMON'S SECOND. Mercenaries, you mean?

MANFRED'S MAN. And professional duelists.

SIMON'S SECOND. Men of negligible character, who make a commerce of honour. It is exactly their ilk I sought to save Sir Simon and your Manfred from.

MANFRED'S MAN. Choose your weapon, sir! You must take the field or Sir Simon will yield.

SIMON'S SECOND. But I have no quarrel with Sir Manfred. I could never bring myself to harm him.

MANFRED'S MAN. It is fortunate, then, that he has already harmed himself. For this morning, I, too, breakfasted with my primary, and when he excused himself to perform his ablutions, it seems he took a tumble in the tub, and thereupon fractured his skull. The man is bedridden, now, and comatose.

SIMON'S SECOND. Well, this is wonderful news! For we may now call off this futile duel!

MANFRED'S MAN. Out of the question, sir.

SIMON'S SECOND. But I should think the quarrel would be forfeit – or at least postponed – both belligerents being absent.

MANFRED'S MAN. Secondry is a sacred contract. We are honour-bound, you and I, to take up the gauntlet on their behalf who cannot take it themselves, due to convenient injury and feigned illness. We must acquit ourselves nobly, lest they be deemed cowards, and we derelicts.

SIMON'S SECOND. Well, if propriety demands that we cross swords, I supposed I shall be more inclined to give you a superficial drubbing than my fellow collegian.

MANFRED'S MAN. Rapiers, then?

SIMON'S SECOND. If you like.

MANFRED'S MAN. No quarter?

SIMON'S SECOND. It shall not need. To your guard, let us conclude this quickly.

(They fight, somewhat matter-of-factly.)

MANFRED'S MAN. I must compliment you, sir! I did not expect to find you so apt with a blade. They must have taught you well at Eton.

SIMON'S SECOND. They did, indeed. But I see you are not altogether unschooled yourself. Westminster?

MANFRED'S MAN. Close to it. St. Cudgel's Penal Academy for Boys, just around the corner.

SIMON'S SECOND. A parochial school? Then how have you become friends with Sir Manfred, who is a devout classist?

MANFRED'S MAN. I have not. For Manfred is no friend, but a client.

SIMON'S SECOND. You mean…?

MANFRED'S MAN. I am a professional duelist, undefeated in 50 documented engagements, and hired by your Manfred to ensure victory in his dispute with Sir Simon.

SIMON'S SECOND. Oh…

*(**MANFRED'S MAN** suddenly presses the attack. But **SIMON'S SECOND** deftly disarms him.)*

SIMON'S SECOND. There! *(hands him back the rapiers)* Well fought.

MANFRED'S MAN. Thank you.

SIMON'S SECOND. You are a mercenary, then? I hope I did not offend you with my earlier remarks. It is impolite to say such things in a person's presence.

MANFRED'S MAN. Not at all, sir. I understood that you meant them to be said behind my back.

SIMON'S SECOND. Will you send Sir Manfred my regards for a rapid recovery?

MANFRED'S MAN. Yes, of course. As you are nearly his friend, I'm sure he will be happy to hear that I spared you on his behalf.

SIMON'S SECOND. That you did what? I bested you. And rather deftly, too.

MANFRED'S MAN. You disarmed me, somewhat, there at the end. But I'm sure I was merely toying with you. Had you not abandoned your weapon and fled the field of battle, there's little question but that I would have recovered my blade forthwith and given you a sound thrashing.

SIMON'S SECOND. I beg your pardon? Fled the field? Is that what you mean to tell Sir Manfred?

MANFRED'S MAN. Not at all, sir. I never repeat such slanders, even when they are true. I shall simply say that I spared you, and leave the details to his imagination.

SIMON'S SECOND. Oh, bosh! *(grabbing a rapier)* Give me that. Come, have at you again. We shall see who is thrashed, and how soundly.

(They fight again, somewhat more vigorously, this time.)

MANFRED'S MAN. This is much better. You fight with more passion.

SIMON'S SECOND. I'm glad you approve.

MANFRED'S MAN. Better for me, that is. I find that an excess of passion saps the skills, and makes one's opponent fight sloppily.

SIMON'S SECOND. Sloppy, am I?

MANFRED'S MAN. I would not say so, sir. Not at all. Your Eton schooling serves you well. I shall have quite a time of defeating you.

SIMON'S SECOND. Defeating me? I did not wish to boast before, but I was, in fact, the finest foilman in my form. You are fortunate I have not peppered you already.

MANFRED'S MAN. Please sir, control your temper.

SIMON'S SECOND. Who are you to tell me to control anything?

MANFRED'S MAN. No one, of course. You are correct, sir. Carry on.

SIMON'S SECOND. I do not need your coaching! *(disarms him)* There!

MANFRED'S MAN. Well done, sir.

SIMON'S SECOND. Do you concede?

MANFRED'S MAN. I must.

SIMON'S SECOND. And have I bested you to your complete satisfaction?

MANFRED'S MAN. Yes, of course.

*(**SIMON'S SECOND** hands over the rapiers, again.)*

MANFRED'S MAN. But it does beg the question…

SIMON'S SECOND. What's that?

MANFRED'S MAN. If we were fighting to the death – per the terms of our duel – and you defeated me – as you seem to believe you have… Why am I still alive?

SIMON'S SECOND. Because I did not wish to slay you. I showed you mercy.

MANFRED'S MAN. So you shirked your duty as a duelist? And betrayed the trust of Sir Simon? No, sir, I will not believe such aspersions.

SIMON'S SECOND. Would you rather I had killed you?

MANFRED'S MAN. Well, it would make the situation considerably less awkward. What shall I tell the papers – or the pub dwellers, for that matter – that won't reflect badly on you, and your family for generations to come?

SIMON'S SECOND. You shall tell them the truth.

MANFRED'S MAN. That you are a coward? No, sir, I cannot. It would be beneath me.

SIMON'S SECOND. I am not a coward!

MANFRED'S MAN. Well, you cannot expect me to believe that you triumphed. We have battled twice now and both times I've come away with your weapon in hand and not a scratch on me.

SIMON'S SECOND. I haven't a scratch either.

MANFRED'S MAN. Clearly, because you fled.

SIMON'S SECOND. *(snatches back his blade)* Give me that. You want a scratch? I shall give you a scratching.

(He attacks.)

MANFRED'S MAN. No, sir, I shall not fight you, sir. Not until you calm down. I am at an unfair advantage when my rivals are rankled. I will not exploit the weakness of a hapless opponent.

SIMON'S SECOND. Hapless, am I?! And weak??

MANFRED'S MAN. You must regain your composure, sir. You are provoked and enraged, therefore prone to mistakes. There's one.

SIMON'S SECOND. Be quiet!

MANFRED'S MAN. And another.

SIMON'S SECOND. I don't need your advice.

MANFRED'S MAN. Certainly not, sir. Shall we fight in silence then?

SIMON'S SECOND. Shut up!

(They fight.)

MANFRED'S MAN. It's no use, sir. I cannot go on with this charade. The whole affair lays us both open to ridicule and derision. Perhaps it were best if I simply apologized and quit the field.

SIMON'S SECOND. This fight will be finished, when I say it is finished!

*(***MANFRED'S MAN*** deftly disarms him, and lays the blade at his throat.)*

SIMON'S SECOND. It is finished.

MANFRED'S MAN. It seems, now, sir, that I have bested you.

SIMON'S SECOND. So it does.

MANFRED'S MAN. But I would not want to presume.

SIMON'S SECOND. What will you do then? Kill me? To verify your victory?

MANFRED'S MAN. Is that what you'd like me to do?

SIMON'S SECOND. No, of course not!

MANFRED'S MAN. You *want* to be spared?

SIMON'S SECOND. Well, of course.

MANFRED'S MAN. I urge you to reconsider. Think of the damage to your reputation. How will you live with the rumours?

SIMON'S SECOND. What rumours?

MANFRED'S MAN. Rumours that you groveled at the feet of a vile honour merchant of negligible character and dubious schooling.

SIMON'S SECOND. I did not grovel!

*(**MANFRED'S MAN** presses the blade to his throat.)*

SIMON'S SECOND. I groveled, I groveled!

MANFRED'S MAN. And begged for your life –

SIMON'S SECOND. Yes, please!

MANFRED'S MAN. And then there's the unmanly weeping –

SIMON'S SECOND. Weeping!?

*(**MANFRED'S MAN** threatens again.)*

SIMON'S SECOND. Yes, yes, I wept, I wept! A complete emotional wreck.

MANFRED'S MAN. Well, then… Do you swear on the grave I have spared you from that I have defeated you in fair accordance with the terms of our duel, and that it is an act of charity for me to let you live at all, for the which you shall be eternally and irrefutably grateful?

SIMON'S SECOND. I do!!

MANFRED'S MAN. *(handing him a legal document and a quill)* Sign here.

SIMON'S SECOND. What's this?

MANFRED'S MAN. Your sworn testament to the groveling and the weeping.

SIMON'S SECOND. You drew this up in advance?

MANFRED'S MAN. I am a professional, after all. There is an old adage, sir: "The pen is mightier than the verbal concession."

*(**SIMON'S SECOND** signs.)*

MANFRED'S MAN. Very good, sir. It has been an honour dishonouring you. And better luck on your second time seconding.

FIN

PHILEON OF ILIUM
IN
THE AMAZON AMBASSADOR

(The Amazon jungle. Enter a **TROJAN DIPLOMAT,** *in search of the Amazon village.)*

PHILEON. What's this? Another castrated kinkajou. And over there, the carcass of a gelded peccary. I daresay I am in the vicinity of the Amazon village! Apollo willing, my diplomatic odyssey to this gods-forsaken continent will soon come to a peaceable fruition.

(Enter, behind him, **DAPHNE,** *an Amazon Sentry.)*

DAPHNE. Who dares to trespass upon the sovereign soil of the Amazon Queen?

PHILEON. Greetings mighty Amazon warrior-ess...tress... person. I am Phileon of Ilium. An emissary of peace from the Kingdom of Troy.

DAPHNE. Ilium? But isn't that... Man country?

PHILEON. Yes, we have both men *and* women, in our country, living together in peaceful coexistence.

DAPHNE. How is that possible? If you have men?

PHILEON. Ahem, yes, well, be that as it may – I bring tidings of peace, and exotic gifts from my King to yours. Queen, that is.

DAPHNE. There can never be peace betwixt Man and Amazon! It is Amazon law.

PHILEON. You have laws against peace?

DAPHNE. We have laws against men. To keep the peace. It is forbidden for any Amazon to speak to a man, or be seen with one, or least of all be one.

PHILEON. What is the punishment?

DAPHNE. Death.

PHILEON. For being a man?

DAPHNE. No, for speaking to a man. The penalty for being a man is… *(has to think about it)* …castration.

PHILEON. What!

DAPHNE. And then death.

PHILEON. *(backing slowly away)* Perhaps, I should go then.

DAPHNE. Not so fast, man-truder! We've got to get you gelded. C'mon, up on the stump.

PHILEON. I'd rather not.

DAPHNE. This won't take a minute. Where did I put that hatchet?

PHILEON. I really – I have other appointments –

DAPHNE. *(drawing a jagged, rusty sword)* This'll have to do.

PHILEON. I gotta go.

(He runs. She blocks his escape.)

DAPHNE. You are spry as a jaguar.

PHILEON. Thanks. Gelding does that.

DAPHNE. You're welcome. Prepare to die.

(She attacks. He tries to fend her off.)

PHILEON. Can't we talk about this? I am a skilled negotiator.

DAPHNE. I told you, Amazon law forbids me to speak to a man.

PHILEON. I could write you a letter. I'm sure I have ink and paper – back in Troy!

DAPHNE. For Nike's sake! Defend yourself!

(She attacks. They fight. He is easily defeated.)

DAPHNE. You fight like a girl.

PHILEON. Coming from a mighty Amazon warrior, I take that as high compliment, indeed.

DAPHNE. No, seriously, like a girl – like a 12-year old girl. I've never seen anyone fight so badly. You should be embarrassed. You're awful.

PHILEON. Well, it's not my area of expertise.

DAPHNE. Killing you isn't even going to be fun.

PHILEON. I don't think you understand. I am an emissary of peace. I did not come here as a fighter. Just the opposite.

DAPHNE. You came here as a lover?

PHILEON. No, as a diplomat!

DAPHNE. Ooh… So you're a bad lover, too?

PHILEON. No, I – That's none of your business!

DAPHNE. Is that why they send you away on long trips?

PHILEON. No! That's not it!!

DAPHNE. Kinda testy for a diplomat. You say you have gifts?

PHILEON. Gifts for the Queen, yes. Golden necklaces. Asian imports.

DAPHNE. Let me see them.

PHILEON. They are for the eyes of the Amazon Queen only.

DAPHNE. How do you know *I'm* not the Amazon Queen?

PHILEON. *Are* you the Amazon Queen?

(Pause. She just stares at him. Another beat, as DAPHNE *checks over her shoulder. Another beat, as she stares at him.)*

DAPHNE. Yes. I am. I am the Amazon Queen.

PHILEON. Then why are you on guard duty?

DAPHNE. Are you calling the Queen a liar?!

PHILEON. No, no, of course not.

DAPHNE. Then bow before me!!

(He does. She likes it.)

Bow before me again! Now, toss your hair.

PHILEON. I apologize, Your Majesty. It's just… I thought you'd be…

DAPHNE. What?

PHILEON. Well… better dressed, for one thing.

DAPHNE. Maybe I would be, if I had some golden necklaces!

PHILEON. Oh, yes, of course. Here you are, Your Majesty. These are Egyptian gold from the finest alchemists in Cairo.

DAPHNE. Oo! Pretty.

PHILEON. And oriental silk from the silk mines of Asia.

DAPHNE. Yay!

PHILEON. And this is chocolate.

DAPHNE. Oh, god, I love you!

PHILEON. What – ?

DAPHNE. Never mind, what else? What else??

PHILEON. That's all for the gifts.

DAPHNE. *(drawing her sword)* Prepare to die.

PHILEON. *(drawing a parchment)* But I also have a message for you, from the King himself.

DAPHNE. All right, let's hear it.

PHILEON. *(reading)* His Royal Majesty craves you –

DAPHNE. He craves me?

PHILEON. To accept these gifts as a token of peace –

DAPHNE. He "craves me" craves me? Or just craves me?

PHILEON. And if it please Your Majesty, the King also desires me –

DAPHNE. He desires *you?*

PHILEON. To establish diplomatic relations –

DAPHNE. What kind of King is he?

PHILEON. And to place myself at your humble service –

DAPHNE. He *desires* you?

PHILEON. To do as Your Highness may please.

DAPHNE. So your King is a homophile?

PHILEON. No!

DAPHNE. It's okay, if he is. We have them here, too.

PHILEON. He's not!

DAPHNE. The next village over is almost all sapphists.

PHILEON. His Majesty is not a sapphist.

DAPHNE. So you are here to please me?

PHILEON. And establish diplomatic relations.

DAPHNE. I see. What is that you are wearing?

PHILEON. What? This tunic?

DAPHNE. Take it off. It displeases me.

PHILEON. Um… You want me to… remove my tunic?

DAPHNE. DO NOT ANGER THE QUEEN!

PHILEON. No, ma'am.

(He hurriedly removes his tunic.)

DAPHNE. Slowly! Slowly! Do not anger the Queen *more slowly.*

(Taking the hint, **PHILEON** *strips off his tunic, slowly and seductively.)*

That's better, yes! O, yes! I see now that there is much that our two civilizations can learn from one another. But if we are going to have relations, you must first master the Amazon Tongue.

PHILEON. Cannot we converse in Latin, the universal language? As we are doing already?

DAPHNE. The Amazon Tongue is much more universal than any *language.*

(She grabs him and kisses him. He flails.)

(Enter **PHOEBE,** *another Amazon Warrior.)*

PHOEBE. Who dares to trespass upon the sovereign soil of the Amazon Queen?

DAPHNE. Not now, Phoebe!

PHOEBE. Daphne? What's going on here??

DAPHNE. Nothing!

PHOEBE. Who is this girl, and what is she doing outside the village?

PHILEON. I'm not a girl.

DAPHNE. Yes, he is. He's a girl. From the next village. We were just experimenting. *(to* **PHILEON***)* Thank you. That was very educational.

PHILEON. I am not a girl! I am Phileon of Ilium, an ambassador of peace, sent by my King to pay respect to the Amazon Queen.

PHOEBE. You're paying *what?*

DAPHNE. Gold and chocolate and silk! And if you keep your voice down, there might be enough for both of us.

PHOEBE. No, no, no, he didn't say gold, he said respect. You were *respecting* her?

PHILEON. Well, yes –

PHOEBE. I want some respect, too!

DAPHNE. You'll have to wait your turn.

PHOEBE. And did you say *chocolate?*

DAPHNE. *(quickly)* All right, fine! You can have some respect. But we're splitting the silk!

PHILEON. Your Majesty, what's going on?

PHOEBE. Her Majesty?? Oh…my…Goddess! You told him you were the Queen! So you could have all the chocolate!!

PHILEON. You're not the Queen?

DAPHNE. Yes, yes, I am! Remove your loincloth! It displeases me, also.

PHOEBE. Don't listen to her, she's not the Queen.

DAPHNE. *(whispers)* Phoebe!! What are you doing?!

PHOEBE. On the contrary, *I* am the Queen! And I am the one your loincloth displeases. Remove it at once.

PHILEON. Now wait a minute –

PHOEBE. I demand respect!

PHILEON. Okay, *what's* going on here?

DAPHNE. You heard the Queen! SHOW SOME RESPECT!!

(He hurriedly undoes his loincloth.)

PHOEBE. Slowly. Show your respect *more slowly.*

(He slowly strips off his loincloth. They squint at him.)

PHOEBE. Hmm… Somehow I thought his respect would be…

DAPHNE. …bigger.

PHOEBE. …wider.

DAPHNE. …ribbed.

PHOEBE. Does he know the Amazon Tongue?

DAPHNE. Yeah, but he's not fluent.

PHILEON. Give me ten minutes.

> (**PHOEBE** *grabs* **PHILEON** *and kisses him. He flails.*)

DAPHNE. All right, that's enough. My turn!

> (**DAPHNE** *pulls* **PHOEBE** *off* **PHILEON** *and kisses him herself.*)

PHOEBE. How dare you lay hands upon your Queen!

> (**PHOEBE** *pulls* **DAPHNE** *off* **PHILEON**.)

DAPHNE. My Queen, my behind!

> (*They fight.*)

PHILEON. Ladies, please! You must not fight. I am here on a peaceful mission. How would it look if I returned to my Kingdom and told them that a civil war broke out among the Amazons, while I was here, because you were all fighting over me, while I stood by naked and helpless and… you know… I'm just going to put my loincloth back on now, if that's okay. Bit nippy here in the Amazon. *(laughs uncomfortably)* I mean, seriously, who knew the tropics could be so drafty? *(picks up his loincloth)* Y'know, maybe the tunic, too.

> (**PHOEBE** *seizes his loincloth. She tries to strangle* **DAPHNE** *with it.*)

PHOEBE. The man-truder is mine!

DAPHNE. I saw him first.

PHOEBE. I saw him naked.

> (*While they fight.* **PHILEON** *tries to cover his privates with a spear, or a palm frond, or a dead kinkajou.*)

> (*Suddenly, the real* **AMAZON QUEEN** *storms in.*)

QUEEN. What in the name of all that is divinely feminine is going on here?

BOTH. Uh oh.

(**PHOEBE** *and* **DAPHNE** *try to hide* **PHILEON**.)

QUEEN. We are trying to have a slumber party in here, and you are going to wake the girls.

PHOEBE. Yes, Your Majesty.

DAPHNE. Sorry, Your Majesty.

PHILEON. Let me guess, now *you're* the Queen.

QUEEN. And what's this?

PHOEBE. A girl. From the next village.

DAPHNE. She was just going home. Off you go!

QUEEN. She doesn't look like a girl…

PHILEON. I am not a girl.

QUEEN. *(aghast)* Oh my Goddess! It's a man!

PHILEON. Thank you.

QUEEN. Is that what all the noise is about? The two of you should be ashamed of yourselves. Fighting over a man.

BOTH. We're sorry.

QUEEN. Now you see why we had to ban them! They are nothing but trouble.

DAPHNE. Yes, but they are a very pretty kind of trouble.

QUEEN. I hope you haven't been teaching him the Amazon tongue.

DAPHNE. No.

PHOEBE. Nuh uh.

DAPHNE. I don't know where he learned it.

QUEEN. I am very disappointed in both of you.

PHOEBE. *(abashed)* You are right, Your Majesty. Men are trouble.

DAPHNE. With a capital tau.

PHOEBE. But we could not help ourselves. Just look at him.

DAPHNE. But first imagine him without the tunic. Take off your tunic!!

PHOEBE. Does not the sight of him make you tingle in ways that you'd rather not talk about in public?

QUEEN. He's not my type.

PHOEBE. Are you kidding? We live in a remote jungle. He's everybody's type.

QUEEN. Some of us know how to show restraint.

DAPHNE. But, Majesty –

PHOEBE. Oh… my… gods!

DAPHNE. What?

PHOEBE. Nobody's that restrained.

DAPHNE. *(realizing)* Holy Hera's teat…!

PHILEON. *(bewildered)* What? What just happened?

PHOEBE. Her Majesty is a sapphist.

QUEEN. *(caught)* No, that's not – Of course not! I have chosen a life of sisterly celibacy because it's fun. And because of the unique educational opportunities.

DAPHNE. O, Your Majesty, for shame!

PHOEBE. We thought you had sworn us all to a life of maiden seclusion and Greco-Roman sportsmanship, out of sisterly affinity. Not just gyno-erotic camaraderie.

QUEEN. But you liked the camaraderie! You all did! Think how much fun we had. The slumber parties and folk songs? Midnight field hockey and flannel womenswear?

PHOEBE. Those are nice. But watch him when he dances. Dance!

PHILEON. If I might say a word –

PHOEBE. Shut up and dance!!

DAPHNE. And he brought us silk!

QUEEN. Now, girls, you mustn't be judgmental. What's wrong with being a sapphist?

PHOEBE. Judgmental? You made us live in a jungle! Eating peccary! When there was chocolate to be had in the city! And shirtless men to bring it to us!

QUEEN. All right, I've heard enough. This is why we don't allow men. One whiff of pheromones and the whole of society crumbles. You're lucky I am a sapphist or there'd be nobody left to do the sensible thing. Now kill him at once. It's for your own good.

DAPHNE. Majesty, please!

QUEEN. *(drawing her sword)* Fine, I'll do it!

PHOEBE. No!!

> *(The* **QUEEN** *attacks* **PHILEON.** **DAPHNE** *and* **PHOEBE** *defend him. They fight.)*

PHILEON. Ladies, women, Amazons. I must insist that you cease fighting at once. And that I be allowed to put on my tunic. We can work this out. I'm sure there's enough of me to go around. Maybe not all the way around. But I'm sure I could manage the two thirds majority necessary to reach an amicable resolution.

QUEEN. Oh, put some clothes on, sausage!

PHOEBE. Don't you dare!

DAPHNE. *(says nothing, but stops to make out with* **PHILEON,** *while the other two fight)*

> *(***PHOEBE** *and* **DAPHNE** *fight the* **QUEEN.** **PHOEBE** *and* **DAPHNE** *fight over* **PHILEON.** *Eventually, the* **QUEEN** *is killed. The fight stops.)*

BOTH. Uh oh…

DAPHNE. Now we're in trouble…

PHOEBE. Hey, wait a minute, I just defeated the Queen in mortal combat. According to Amazon law, that makes me the new Queen!

PHILEON. It does?

DAPHNE. Hold on, I defeated her, too. *(to* **PHILEON***)* You're my witness.

PHOEBE. Not if I pluck his eyes out.

> *(***PHOEBE** *attacks* **PHILEON.** **DAPHNE** *defends him. They fight.)*

PHOEBE. You just want more chocolate!

DAPHNE. You're not the only one sick of peccary!

> *(They fight.)*

PHILEON. Wait – If I could just – Ladies – I beg of you – Excuse me – Hello –

(In the end, **PHOEBE** *is killed, and* **DAPHNE** *mortally wounded.)*

PHILEON. Ohhh, this looks bad…

DAPHNE. Is she dead?

PHILEON. Now you really are the Amazon Queen. Congratulations.

DAPHNE. It is well. Come here, man-truder… Heed my dying wish.

PHILEON. You're not going to kiss me again?

DAPHNE. Is that all you men think about?

PHILEON. All *we* think about?!

DAPHNE. You have brought strife and carnage to this tranquil Amazon village.

PHILEON. And I am *so* sorry about that.

DAPHNE. Return to your King. Tell him there can never be peace between our peoples. It is the only way.

PHILEON. Yes, yes. I see that now.

DAPHNE. Man-truder –

PHILEON. Yes, Majesty?

DAPHNE. Now I'm going to kiss you.

(She grabs him and kisses him. He flails.)

FIN

CPSIA information can be obtained at www.ICGtesting.com
Printed in the USA
BVOW021125030313

314603BV00006B/49/P